jB
ROOSEVEL
T

McAuley, Karen.

Eleanor Roosevelt.

$17.95

DATE		
FEB 19 1992		
MAR 18 1992		
MAR 31 1993		
MAR 2 3 1994		
JUN 2 1 1994		
OCT 19 1994		
DEC 2 3 1995		

$5.00 FEE PLUS FULL PRICE
FOR EACH ITEM LOST

WILLITS BRANCH LIBRARY

© THE BAKER & TAYLOR CO.

ELEANOR ROOSEVELT

ELEANOR ROOSEVELT

Karen McAuley

CHELSEA HOUSE PUBLISHERS
NEW YORK
PHILADELPHIA

EDITORIAL DIRECTOR: Nancy Toff
SENIOR EDITOR: John W. Selfridge
ASSOCIATE EDITOR: Marian W. Taylor
MANAGING EDITOR: Karyn Gullen Browne
COPY CHIEF: Perry King
EDITORIAL STAFF: Maria Behan, Karen Dreste,
　　　　　　　　Pierre Hauser, Kathleen McDermott,
　　　　　　　　Howard Ratner, Alma Rodriguez-Sokol,
　　　　　　　　Bert Yaeger
PICTURE EDITOR: Elizabeth Terhune
PICTURE RESEARCH: Emily Miller, Matthew Miller
ART DIRECTOR: Giannella Garrett
LAYOUT: Irene Friedman
ART ASSISTANTS: Noreen Lamb, Carol McDougall,
　　　　　　　　Victoria Tomaselli
COVER ILLUSTRATION: Kye Carbone

Frontispiece courtesy of AP/Wide World

3 5 7 9 8 6 4 2

Library of Congress Cataloging in Publication Data

McAuley, Karen. ELEANOR ROOSEVELT.

(World leaders past & present)
Bibliography: p.
Includes index.
1. Roosevelt, Eleanor, 1884–1962 — Juvenile literature.
2. Presidents — United States — Wives — Biography —
Juvenile literature. [1. Roosevelt, Eleanor, 1884–1962.
2. First ladies]
I. Title. II. Series.
E807.1.R48M35　　1987　　973.917′092′4　[B]　86-21612

ISBN 0-87754-574-X
　　0-7910-0598-4 (pbk.)

Contents

John Adams
John Quincy Adams
Konrad Adenauer
Alexander the Great
Salvador Allende
Marc Antony
Corazon Aquino
Yasir Arafat
King Arthur
Hafez al-Assad
Kemal Atatürk
Attila
Clement Attlee
Augustus Caesar
Menachem Begin
David Ben-Gurion
Otto von Bismarck
Léon Blum
Simon Bolívar
Cesare Borgia
Willy Brandt
Leonid Brezhnev
Julius Caesar
John Calvin
Jimmy Carter
Fidel Castro
Catherine the Great
Charlemagne
Chiang Kai-Shek
Winston Churchill
Georges Clemenceau
Cleopatra
Constantine the Great
Hernán Cortés
Oliver Cromwell
Georges-Jacques
   Danton
Jefferson Davis
Moshe Dayan
Charles de Gaulle
Eamon De Valera
Eugene Debs
Deng Xiaoping
Benjamin Disraeli
Alexander Dubček
François & Jean-Claude
   Duvalier
Dwight Eisenhower
Eleanor of Aquitaine
Elizabeth I
Faisal
Ferdinand & Isabella
Francisco Franco
Benjamin Franklin

Frederick the Great
Indira Gandhi
Mohandas Gandhi
Giuseppe Garibaldi
Amin & Bashir Gemayel
Genghis Khan
William Gladstone
Mikhail Gorbachev
Ulysses S. Grant
Ernesto "Che" Guevara
Tenzin Gyatso
Alexander Hamilton
Dag Hammarskjöld
Henry VIII
Henry of Navarre
Paul von Hindenburg
Hirohito
Adolf Hitler
Ho Chi Minh
King Hussein
Ivan the Terrible
Andrew Jackson
James I
Wojciech Jaruzelski
Thomas Jefferson
Joan of Arc
Pope John XXIII
Pope John Paul II
Lyndon Johnson
Benito Juárez
John Kennedy
Robert Kennedy
Jomo Kenyatta
Ayatollah Khomeini
Nikita Khrushchev
Kim Il Sung
Martin Luther King, Jr.
Henry Kissinger
Kublai Khan
Lafayette
Robert E. Lee
Vladimir Lenin
Abraham Lincoln
David Lloyd George
Louis XIV
Martin Luther
Judas Maccabeus
James Madison
Nelson & Winnie
   Mandela
Mao Zedong
Ferdinand Marcos
George Marshall

Mary, Queen of Scots
Tomáš Masaryk
Golda Meir
Klemens von Metternich
James Monroe
Hosni Mubarak
Robert Mugabe
Benito Mussolini
Napoléon Bonaparte
Gamal Abdel Nasser
Jawaharlal Nehru
Nero
Nicholas II
Richard Nixon
Kwame Nkrumah
Daniel Ortega
Mohammed Reza Pahlavi
Thomas Paine
Charles Stewart
   Parnell
Pericles
Juan Perón
Peter the Great
Pol Pot
Muammar el-Qaddafi
Ronald Reagan
Cardinal Richelieu
Maximilien Robespierre
Eleanor Roosevelt
Franklin Roosevelt
Theodore Roosevelt
Anwar Sadat
Haile Selassie
Prince Sihanouk
Jan Smuts
Joseph Stalin
Sukarno
Sun Yat-sen
Tamerlane
Mother Teresa
Margaret Thatcher
Josip Broz Tito
Toussaint L'Ouverture
Leon Trotsky
Pierre Trudeau
Harry Truman
Queen Victoria
Lech Walesa
George Washington
Chaim Weizmann
Woodrow Wilson
Xerxes
Emiliano Zapata
Zhou Enlai

CHELSEA HOUSE PUBLISHERS

ON LEADERSHIP
Arthur M. Schlesinger, jr.

LEADERSHIP, it may be said, is really what makes the world go round. Love no doubt smooths the passage; but love is a private transaction between consenting adults. Leadership is a public transaction with history. The idea of leadership affirms the capacity of individuals to move, inspire, and mobilize masses of people so that they act together in pursuit of an end. Sometimes leadership serves good purposes, sometimes bad; but whether the end is benign or evil, great leaders are those men and women who leave their personal stamp on history.

Now, the very concept of leadership implies the proposition that individuals can make a difference. This proposition has never been universally accepted. From classical times to the present day, eminent thinkers have regarded individuals as no more than the agents and pawns of larger forces, whether the gods and goddesses of the ancient world or, in the modern era, race, class, nation, the dialectic, the will of the people, the spirit of the times, history itself. Against such forces, the individual dwindles into insignificance.

So contends the thesis of historical determinism. Tolstoy's great novel *War and Peace* offers a famous statement of the case. Why, Tolstoy asked, did millions of men in the Napoleonic wars, denying their human feelings and their common sense, move back and forth across Europe slaughtering their fellows? "The war," Tolstoy answered, "was bound to happen simply because it was bound to happen." All prior history predetermined it. As for leaders, they, Tolstoy said, "are but the labels that serve to give a name to an end and, like labels, they have the least possible connection with the event." The greater the leader, "the more conspicuous the inevitability and the predestination of every act he commits." The leader, said Tolstoy, is "the slave of history."

Determinism takes many forms. Marxism is the determinism of class. Nazism the determinism of race. But the idea of men and women as the slaves of history runs athwart the deepest human instincts. Rigid determinism abolishes the idea of human freedom—

the assumption of free choice that underlies every move we make, every word we speak, every thought we think. It abolishes the idea of human responsibility, since it is manifestly unfair to reward or punish people for actions that are by definition beyond their control. No one can live consistently by any deterministic creed. The Marxist states prove this themselves by their extreme susceptibility to the cult of leadership.

More than that, history refutes the idea that individuals make no difference. In December 1931 a British politician crossing Park Avenue in New York City between 76th and 77th Streets around 10:30 P.M. looked in the wrong direction and was knocked down by an automobile—a moment, he later recalled, of a man aghast, a world aglare: "I do not understand why I was not broken like an eggshell or squashed like a gooseberry." Fourteen months later an American politician, sitting in an open car in Miami, Florida, was fired on by an assassin; the man beside him was hit. Those who believe that individuals make no difference to history might well ponder whether the next two decades would have been the same had Mario Constasino's car killed Winston Churchill in 1931 and Giuseppe Zangara's bullet killed Franklin Roosevelt in 1933. Suppose, in addition, that Adolf Hitler had been killed in the street fighting during the Munich *Putsch* of 1923 and that Lenin had died of typhus during World War I. What would the 20th century be like now?

For better or for worse, individuals do make a difference. "The notion that a people can run itself and its affairs anonymously," wrote the philosopher William James, "is now well known to be the silliest of absurdities. Mankind does nothing save through initiatives on the part of inventors, great or small, and imitation by the rest of us—these are the sole factors in human progress. Individuals of genius show the way, and set the patterns, which common people then adopt and follow."

Leadership, James suggests, means leadership in thought as well as in action. In the long run, leaders in thought may well make the greater difference to the world. But, as Woodrow Wilson once said, "Those only are leaders of men, in the general eye, who lead in action. . . . It is at their hands that new thought gets its translation into the crude language of deeds." Leaders in thought often invent in solitude and obscurity, leaving to later generations the tasks of imitation. Leaders in action—the leaders portrayed in this series—have to be effective in their own time.

And they cannot be effective by themselves. They must act in response to the rhythms of their age. Their genius must be adapted, in a phrase of William James's, "to the receptivities of the moment." Leaders are useless without followers. "There goes the mob," said the French politician hearing a clamor in the streets. "I am their leader. I must follow them." Great leaders turn the inchoate emotions of the mob to purposes of their own. They seize on the opportunities of their time, the hopes, fears, frustrations, crises, potentialities. They succeed when events have prepared the way for them, when the community is awaiting to be aroused, when they can provide the clarifying and organizing ideas. Leadership ignites the circuit between the individual and the mass and thereby alters history.

It may alter history for better or for worse. Leaders have been responsible for the most extravagant follies and most monstrous crimes that have beset suffering humanity. They have also been vital in such gains as humanity has made in individual freedom, religious and racial tolerance, social justice and respect for human rights.

There is no sure way to tell in advance who is going to lead for good and who for evil. But a glance at the gallery of men and women in *World Leaders—Past and Present* suggests some useful tests.

One test is this: do leaders lead by force or by persuasion? By command or by consent? Through most of history leadership was exercised by the divine right of authority. The duty of followers was to defer and to obey. "Theirs not to reason why,/ Theirs but to do and die." On occasion, as with the so-called "enlightened despots" of the 18th century in Europe, absolutist leadership was animated by humane purposes. More often, absolutism nourished the passion for domination, land, gold and conquest and resulted in tyranny.

The great revolution of modern times has been the revolution of equality. The idea that all people should be equal in their legal condition has undermined the old structure of authority, hierarchy and deference. The revolution of equality has had two contrary effects on the nature of leadership. For equality, as Alexis de Tocqueville pointed out in his great study *Democracy in America*, might mean equality in servitude as well as equality in freedom.

"I know of only two methods of establishing equality in the political world," Tocqueville wrote. "Rights must be given to every citizen, or none at all to anyone . . . save one, who is the master of all." There was no middle ground "between the sovereignty of all and the absolute power of one man." In his astonishing prediction of 20th-century totalitarian dictatorship, Tocqueville explained how the revolution of equality could lead to the *"Führerprinzip"* and more terrible absolutism than the world had ever known.

But when rights are given to every citizen and the sovereignty of all is established, the problem of leadership takes a new form, becomes more exacting than ever before. It is easy to issue commands and enforce them by the rope and the stake, the concentration camp and the *gulag.* It is much harder to use argument and achievement to overcome opposition and win consent. The Founding Fathers of the United States understood the difficulty. They believed that history had given them the opportunity to decide, as Alexander Hamilton wrote in the first Federalist Paper, whether men are indeed capable of basing government on "reflection and choice, or whether they are forever destined to depend . . . on accident and force."

Government by reflection and choice called for a new style of leadership and a new quality of followership. It required leaders to be responsive to popular concerns, and it required followers to be active and informed participants in the process. Democracy does not eliminate emotion from politics; sometimes it fosters demagoguery; but it is confident that, as the greatest of democratic leaders put it, you cannot fool all of the people all of the time. It measures leadership by results and retires those who overreach or falter or fail.

It is true that in the long run despots are measured by results too. But they can postpone the day of judgment, sometimes indefinitely, and in the meantime they can do infinite harm. It is also true that democracy is no guarantee of virtue and intelligence in government, for the voice of the people is not necessarily the voice of God. But democracy, by assuring the right of opposition, offers built-in resistance to the evils inherent in absolutism. As the theologian Reinhold Niebuhr summed it up, "Man's capacity for justice makes democracy possible, but man's inclination to injustice makes democracy necessary."

A second test for leadership is the end for which power is sought. When leaders have as their goal the supremacy of a master race or the promotion of totalitarian revolution or the acquisition and exploitation of colonies or the protection of greed and privilege or the preservation of personal power, it is likely that their leadership will do little to advance the cause of humanity. When their goal is the abolition of slavery, the liberation of women, the enlargement of opportunity for the poor and powerless, the extension of equal rights to racial minorities, the defense of the freedoms of expression and opposition, it is likely that their leadership will increase the sum of human liberty and welfare.

Leaders have done great harm to the world. They have also conferred great benefits. You will find both sorts in this series. Even "good" leaders must be regarded with a certain wariness. Leaders are not demigods; they put on their trousers one leg after another just like ordinary mortals. No leader is infallible, and every leader needs to be reminded of this at regular intervals. Irreverence irritates leaders but is their salvation. Unquestioning submission corrupts leaders and demands followers. Making a cult of a leader is always a mistake. Fortunately hero worship generates its own antidote. "Every hero," said Emerson, "becomes a bore at last."

The signal benefit the great leaders confer is to embolden the rest of us to live according to our own best selves, to be active, insistent, and resolute in affirming our own sense of things. For great leaders attest to the reality of human freedom against the supposed inevitabilities of history. And they attest to the wisdom and power that may lie within the most unlikely of us, which is why Abraham Lincoln remains the supreme example of great leadership. A great leader, said Emerson, exhibits new possibilities to all humanity. "We feed on genius. . . . Great men exist that there may be greater men."

Great leaders, in short, justify themselves by emancipating and empowering their followers. So humanity struggles to master its destiny, remembering with Alexis de Tocqueville: "It is true that around every man a fatal circle is traced beyond which he cannot pass; but within the wide verge of that circle he is powerful and free; as it is with man, so with communities."

—*New York*

1

A Victory for People Everywhere

It had been dark for hours outside the Palais de Chaillot in Paris, when the voting started. Eleanor Roosevelt sat listening. For more than two years she had worked on the International Declaration of Human Rights. Now the document needed to be approved by the United Nations General Assembly.

"Article 1," the president of the assembly called out. "All human beings are born free and equal in dignity and rights. They are endowed by nature with reason and conscience, and should act towards one another in a spirit of brotherhood."

The tension in the room lessened as one delegation after another approved the articles. Eleanor scanned the tired faces of the members of the General Assembly.

"Article 5: Everyone has the right to recognition, everywhere, as a person before the law," the president continued.

Eleanor remembered how pleased she had been to be asked to serve on the commission. She was delighted to accept because she was determined to prove that the UN could help secure greater rights for people all over the world.

Her great contribution was her persistence in carrying into practice her deep belief in liberty and equality. She would not accept that anyone should suffer — because they were women, or children, or foreign, or poor, or stateless refugees.
—JEAN MONNET
French economist and diplomat, recommending Eleanor Roosevelt for the Nobel Peace Prize

Eleanor Roosevelt as the U.S. delegate to the UN Commission on Human Rights, giving a press conference on April 14, 1952. Eleanor was chair of the commission for five years after being appointed by President Harry Truman in 1945. By the end of her long career of service, Eleanor was one of the best-known and most well-loved women in the world.

German refugees leaving war-torn Aachen in 1944. It was left, in the words of one American observer, "as dead as a Roman ruin." Against the background of ravaged Europe, with its millions of displaced persons, the International Human Rights Charter was passed, containing guarantees of the rights of every human being.

I do not feel that we, as individuals, or as a nation, gain either dignity or prestige by refusing to know the people who lead the great opposition to our way of life.

—ELEANOR ROOSEVELT
from her autobiography

After being unanimously elected chair of the commission, she spent hundreds of hours at the conference table with the delegates. They represented so many different ideologies that she often had to struggle to get them to agree upon the wording of some of the 26 articles. At times she had appealed to them from her own humility. "I am probably the least learned person around this table," she explained, "so I have thought of this article in terms of what the ordinary person would understand." At other times she flattered them into letting go of their objections. "I am sure there is a great deal to be said for your arguments," she nodded, "but don't you think it would be a good idea if . . ." And when the delegates had indulged themselves in angry harangues, she glowered and pounded her gavel.

In her mid-sixties Eleanor Roosevelt was as energetic and strong as a young woman. She walked so quickly that colleagues frequently had trouble keeping up with her, and her habit of hard work was so ingrained that she hardly noticed the rigorous schedule she set for the commission. Members far younger than she complained. When they asked for shorter sessions, she simply told them to shorten their speeches. "No one can ever tell me that women like to talk longer than men!" she exclaimed.

In fact, she thought, getting the commission to draft a single meaningful document had taken more patience and been harder work than raising her five children. Yet she had pressed on for more than two years and 85 meetings, fueled by her powerful conviction that people in all countries all over the world must be allowed to live with dignity and freedom, safe from persecution. The main stumbling block had been that the Soviets had wanted the document to describe the duties people owed their governments in exchange for jobs, education, and health care, while representatives of democratic countries felt it should simply describe human needs and de-

Eleanor holding the Universal Declaration of Human Rights in 1949. Not a law or treaty, the declaration is a standard of achievement that is still used to measure the adherence of member states to the principles of the United Nations Charter.

fine the rights and freedoms all people should have no matter where they lived.

As the voting went on, it became apparent that the Soviet Union and its allies would be overruled, so they abstained. So did Saudi Arabia and the Union of South Africa. When at a few minutes after midnight the roll was complete the other members of the United Nations General Assembly had unanimously approved the declaration.

Leaving the meeting in the early morning of December 10, 1948, Eleanor was already thinking about the work ahead. For years she would work to try to establish international laws to protect the rights outlined in the declaration. And though that job would not be finished when she left the UN in 1952, the declaration itself would have an impact in the writing of laws, treaties, and constitutions of nations all over the world.

Eleanor Roosevelt, whom some called the "First Lady of the World" worked most of her life helping others. She knew firsthand about the struggle for human dignity, and though she remained humble and compassionate, she was one of the most powerful women in the world.

Anna Eleanor Roosevelt was born on October 11, 1884. She was the first child born to a popular young couple in New York City's most elegant society. Eleanor's mother, Anna Hall, was a minister's daughter and the product of a strict upbringing. An attractive young woman, she was the center of attention at many of the parties she attended. Eleanor's father, Elliott Roosevelt, was a handsome, fun-loving sportsman. As a child he had been sickly, but nonetheless adventuresome, and by the time he was a young man he had learned to hunt and ride. He even stalked tigers in India with his older brother Theodore, who later would become the 26th president of the United States.

Though Elliott Roosevelt was somewhat impetuous and irresponsible, to his daughter he was perfect. He was "the one great love of my life as a child," she confessed. "I loved the way he treated me . . . and I never doubted that I stood first in his heart."

I was a shy, solemn child even at the age of two, and I am sure that even when I danced I never smiled. My earliest recollections are of being dressed up and allowed to come down to dance for a group of gentlemen who applauded and laughed as I pirouetted before them.

—ELEANOR ROOSEVELT
from her autobiography

The little girl felt very differently about her mother. She was awed by the young woman's beauty. As a toddler, Eleanor would stand solemnly in the doorway waiting for her mother to acknowledge her. Long after, when Eleanor was a grown woman, it still hurt her to remember "the look in her eyes and . . . the tone in her voice as she said, 'Come in Granny.'" Her mother's teasing nickname for her shamed the little girl, and for the rest of her life she felt awkward and homely.

Like most children of wealthy families, Eleanor and her younger brother, Elliott, Jr., were tended by nurses and governesses. They spent little time with their parents, yet by the age of five Eleanor was aware that somehow her father was having problems. Nothing was said to her directly, but from bits of adult conversations she learned, as she later wrote in her autobiography, that "something was wrong with my father and from my point of view nothing could be wrong with him."

In fact, Elliott drank. He seemed to like nothing better than being off with his friends hunting, yachting, and drinking. At home he was moody and difficult. Like most people at the time, the Roosevelts firmly believed that alcoholism was a form of moral weakness. The family banished him from their sight when he lost control. Young Eleanor was confused and hurt when she found the parent she adored gone without explanation.

While her father was away, Eleanor slept in her mother's room. She loved to watch her get ready to go out in the evenings. Years later she wrote, "She looked so beautiful I was grateful to be allowed to touch her dress or her jewels or anything that was part of the vision which I admired inordinately."

Trying to keep Elliott with the family, but remove the temptation of his regular drinking friends, the Roosevelts traveled to Europe. In 1891, when Anna was pregnant with Hall, their last child, the couple rented a house just outside Paris. Elliott escaped for days at a time to live with another woman. When they returned to New York, Anna discovered yet another disgrace. Katy Mann, a pretty young housekeeper who had had a new baby while working for

Eleanor at age three in Huntington, New York, 1887. A quiet, unhappy child, Eleanor retained painful memories of her mother teasingly nicknaming her "Granny." Her slow emergence from the bonds of shyness became a process of self-discovery that helped form the selfless compassion seen throughout her adulthood.

Anna Hall Roosevelt, Eleanor's mother. Beautiful, intelligent, and society-
minded, Anna was unhappily
married, and she died when
Eleanor was eight. Feeling
spurned by her mother,
Eleanor developed a deep attachment to her father, an
unreliable eccentric who was
all but banished from the
family until his death when
Eleanor was 10.

the Roosevelts, had gone to the family lawyers and
threatened to reveal publicly that Elliott was the
child's father if the family did not support them.

Elliott's brother, Theodore, who was then a politically ambitious public service commissioner, was
furious. His brother's scandalous behavior could
not only ruin his career, but proved to him that
Elliott was "a maniac morally as well as mentally,"
and "a flagrant man-swine."

Seeking comfort, Anna took the children to Bar
Harbor, Maine, for a summer with their aunts and
uncles while Elliott was sent off to manage one of
his brothers-in-law's coal mines in a small town in
Virginia. Away from the angry disapproval of his
family, Elliott became known as a lively eccentric
who was inclined to perform daredevil stunts like
riding horses across railroad trestles in the paths
of oncoming trains.

In the autumn Anna returned to New York with
the children. Eleanor, a tall, willowy eight-year-old,
was so painfully withdrawn that her mother was
concerned. She tried to draw her daughter out with
extra attention, but Eleanor still felt alone and aban-
doned. She could not understand why her father
had been sent away.

That winter, when Anna became sick, Eleanor
was moved by her suffering. For hours she sat by
her mother's side and silently stroked her aching
head. Eleanor later remembered that "feeling that I
was useful was perhaps the greatest joy I experienced." For the rest of her life the satisfaction of
helping others would remain one of her greatest
pleasures.

When Anna's illness worsened in 1892, Eleanor
and her brothers were sent to stay with relatives.
Their father begged to be allowed to visit his sick
wife, but his angry mother-in-law refused to let him.
By the time Elliott was able to return, his wife was
dead, and his mother-in-law had been made legal
guardian of his children.

Eleanor and her brothers, Elliott, Jr., and Hall,
were no sooner moved into their grandmother's New
York City brownstone, when their father visited. "I
remember going down into the high-ceilinged, dim

library on the first floor of the house on West 37th Street," she wrote. "He sat in a big chair. He was dressed all in black, looking very sad. He held out his arms and gathered me to him. In a little while he began to talk, to explain to me that my mother was gone, that she had been all the world to him, that now he had only my brothers and myself, that my brothers were very young, and that he and I must keep close together. Someday I would make a home for him again, we would travel together and do many things. . . ."

"Somehow it was always he and I. I did not understand whether my brothers were to be our children or whether he felt that they would be going to a school and later be independent."

"There started that day a feeling which never left me, that he and I were very close and someday would have a life of our own together. He told me to write to him often, to be a good girl, not to give any trouble, to study hard, to grow up into a woman he could be proud of, and he would come to see me whenever it was possible."

Elliott played upon his daughter's romantic dreams of him, yet he seldom visited. His letters were filled with promises, and Eleanor cherished

Three homeless children in a New York tenement, photographed by the great reformer Jacob Riis. Eleanor's childhood, though unhappy, was luxurious when compared with the lives of the immigrants pouring into America. The disparity remained prominent in Eleanor's consciousness throughout her career.

Eleanor (right) with her favorite brother, "Little Ellie" (Elliott). "He was so good, he never had to be reproved," she once said. Young Elliot died of scarlet fever when Eleanor was nine, which added to her sense of loss.

UPI/BETTMANN NEWSPHOTOS

and saved them.

The following spring Eleanor's brother Elliott, Jr., died after a struggle with scarlet fever and diphtheria. There was little comfort left for Eleanor. Grandmother Hall was a strict disciplinarian with her grandchildren. She was determined to have them grow up to become upright, productive adults, unlike her own children. Her son, Vallie, who still lived at home, was a gloomy alcoholic who was occasionally violent. Her daughter, Edith, affectionately called "Pussie," who also lived at home, was a stormy, passionate young woman who suffered wild romantic crushes.

Though Elliott's visits were irregular, in her heart Eleanor clung to her father. "Subconsciously, I must always have been waiting for his visits," she wrote, "never was I in the house, even in my room two long flights of stairs above the entrance door, that I did not hear his voice the minute he entered the front door. Walking downstairs was far too slow. I slid down the bannisters and usually catapulted into his arms before his hat was hung up."

After the death of Elliott, Jr., Eleanor's father wrote her less often and became even less reliable. Yet Eleanor's love for him remained strong. She even forgave him the time when they were out walking his dogs and he excused himself to go into the Knickerbocker Club, leaving her and the terriers with the doorman. Six hours later, he returned to her so drunk that he had to be bundled into a cab by the club's porters.

This incident so outraged Grandmother Hall that she thoroughly discouraged her son-in-law's visits. So Elliott came to New York without telling anyone and eventually rented a house on 102nd Street, where he lived with a woman. Though the house was less than three miles away from his daughter, she rarely saw him. He became increasingly anxious and erratic, and was drunk more often. In the summer of 1894 Elliott died after falling out of an upper-story window of his home.

Eleanor cried herself to sleep, but in her heart she refused to believe her father was dead. In her autobiography she explained that somehow she "began the next day living in her dreamworld as usual. . . . I lived with him more closely, probably, than I had when he was alive."

Her father's image remained with her all her life, both a source of great strength and of terrible weakness. While she was determined to become the unselfish, generous, cheerful woman he wanted her to be, within her she raged at the man who had broken so many promises. Her idealization of him and her anger confused her perceptions of people and left her feeling that love could not be trusted to last.

> *Eleanor was born into a secure golden world in which significant or even ominous events around the globe were hardly noticed.*
> —JOSEPH P. LASH
> journalist and biographer

UPI/BETTMANN NEWSPHOTOS

Elliott Roosevelt, Sr., with Eleanor (right) and her brothers (left to right) Hall and Elliott. Eleanor's father was an alcoholic who was replaced as the children's guardian by their grandmother after their mother's death in December 1892.

2

A New Life

For the next five years Eleanor and Hall lived with their grandmother and her grown children in New York City. The house was dark and formal. Off its narrow front hallway, which was lit by a single gas lamp, were several gloomy rooms, but there was no place for children to play. Grandmother Hall dutifully saw that Eleanor continued the schooling she had begun a few years earlier. In classes with a few other girls she read poetry, Greek and Roman history, and continued to study French, which she had begun learning as a young child. These studies and dance classes were considered education enough for a young woman at that time.

For Eleanor the dance classes were excruciating. Not only was she shy and awkward, but her clothes were odd. Grandmother Hall had no idea what girls Eleanor's age were wearing, so while the others' long skirts swirled gracefully around their ankles, Eleanor's did not even cover her knees.

The best part of young Eleanor's life with her grandmother were the summers, when the family moved to their spacious home on the Hudson River in Tivoli, New York. When she was not daydreaming

Poor child, she has had so much sorrow crowded into her short life she now takes everything very quietly.
—MARY LUDLOW HALL
Eleanor's grandmother, on Eleanor shortly after her father's death

Portrait of Eleanor from her Allenswood school album, taken in 1898, when she was 15 years old. Eleanor found a mentor in the headmistress there, Marie Souvestre, who gave the young girl a standard of morality and intellectual achievement she would cherish her entire life.

23

or nestled with a book in a tree, Eleanor caught tadpoles or made up games with her little brother Hall, who was six years her junior. She also rode her pony. Rarely was there anyone her own age to play with. During those summers Eleanor read almost every book in her grandmother's extensive library.

The children saw little of their father's family, though they did see their Uncle Ted and Aunt Edith in Oyster Bay once or twice during the summer and spent part of every Christmas holiday with Aunt Corrine. Family visits were always a challenge for Eleanor. Amid what must have seemed to be crowds of confident cousins, she was suddenly expected to play unfamiliar and sometimes rough games. Uncle Ted, always a boy at heart, led the children on noisy parades, chased them through haystacks, or rolled with them down steep hills. Sometimes they even went camping. Though such spirited play made Eleanor feel clumsy and inadequate, her uncle's sociability and playfulness always appealed to her.

Eleanor saw boys her own age only rarely, and thus felt very shy with them. One Christmas there

A young Eleanor with her pony. At her grandmother's estate in Tivoli, overlooking the Hudson River, Eleanor participated in fitting activities for a young, well-bred girl, including riding, reading, dancing classes, and family visits.

AP/WIDE WORLD PHOTO

Franklin D. Roosevelt (top center), Eleanor's distant cousin and future husband, as manager of a baseball team at Groton, the elite prep school that all the Roosevelt men attended. Eleanor was delighted with her handsome cousin's attentions, although some of her relatives thought she could do better.

was a dance at which Eleanor mingled with other young people. Eleanor felt ugly, however, so she was grateful when handsome, 16-year-old Franklin, a distant cousin, asked her to dance. In fact, a photograph of Eleanor taken at about this time, shows that she was attractive, with beautiful eyes and shining, upswept hair.

Almost 15, Eleanor went off to school in England. Grandmother Hall may have decided to send her away to protect her from Uncle Vallie's constant drinking or Aunt Pussie's stormy moods. Or perhaps the older woman remembered that her daughter wanted her children to be better educated than she was. In any case, Eleanor's grandmother chose Allenswood, a small school for girls, outside of London. Its headmistress, Mademoiselle Marie Souvestre, had long been a family friend.

From the moment Eleanor arrived in the autumn

of 1899, the headmistress took an interest in her. The sheltered, melancholy girl was drawn to the vibrant woman. Mademoiselle Souvestre was a lively, energetic, unconventional teacher, who loved life and enjoyed her students. She was determined to make all of them think for themselves. Eleanor had never met anyone like her. "Sou," as she was called affectionately, thrived on life's challenges and believed everyone had the responsibility to try to make the world a better place. Eleanor adored her.

Though life at Allenswood was strict and far from luxurious, Eleanor loved it. Physical beauty and social graces were unimportant there. Instead, loyalty and originality were the highest values. Eleanor's quick mind and willingness to help others made her a favorite of students and faculty alike. Years later, she wrote, "I felt that I was starting a new life, free from all my former sins and traditions . . . this was the first time in my life that my fears left me. If I lived up to the rules and told the truth there was nothing to fear." At Allenswood anything seemed possible — Eleanor even joined the school's field hockey team.

In 1901 Eleanor and Mademoiselle Souvestre spent spring vacation traveling together in France and Italy. The trip, the first of two journeys with her beloved teacher, was "one of the most momentous things that ever happened in my education" she wrote, "[and] was a revelation." From Sou, Eleanor came to love traveling. She learned to explore on her own, to eat local foods, and to visit places not usually seen by tourists. Mademoiselle Souvestre made her responsible for making all their travel arrangements and Eleanor felt proud of her efficiency at organizing them. The young woman bloomed.

According to her cousin Corrine Robinson, who entered Allenswood two and one-half years after Eleanor arrived, Eleanor had become "the most important person at the school" and the headmistress's "supreme favorite," but somehow no one was jealous of her. The older girl was a kind of honorary staff member, who helped other girls with their studies and made everyone feel at home. Eleanor was a natural, enthusiastic teacher. The admiration

Eleanor's Uncle Vallie (Valentine) Hall. He lived with his mother and niece, and was an alcoholic who later became quite insane. Appalled by her uncle's drunken scenes, which evoked memories of her father, Eleanor retreated behind a wall of rigid self-control.

she received at Allenswood nourished and strengthened her.

After three of the happiest years in her life, Eleanor reluctantly returned to New York. She was nearly 18 and Grandmother Hall insisted that it was time for her to make her debut into society.

Life in the Hall household had deteriorated dramatically. Vallie's drinking had made him angry and sick. He often stormed through the house looking for fights. Sometimes he would crouch in the attic with a shotgun and fire out the windows at anyone who happened to be on the lawn. Terrified, but unable to control him, Grandmother Hall had almost completely withdrawn to her room. Naturally, visitors had stopped coming.

Uncle Vallie's drunken rages disturbed Eleanor. "This period," she later wrote, "was my first real contact with anyone who had completely lost the power of self-control," but of course it was not. Though she could never acknowledge it, Vallie's drinking spells probably reminded her of her father's. This fear of lack of control made her develop her own self-control. Much of the liveliness she had

Some people consider ambition a sin but it seems to me to be a great good for it leads one to do and to be things which without it one could never have been.
—ELEANOR ROOSEVELT
from an essay she
wrote at 14

Marie Souvestre, headmistress at Allenswood, a stylish finishing school on the outskirts of London. Mlle. Souvestre prodded Eleanor intellectually and emotionally in order to make the young girl understand her obligations to people less fortunate than herself.

I have not found her easily influenced in anything that was not perfectly straightforward and honest, but I often found she influenced others in the right direction.
—MADEMOISELLE SOUVESTRE
headmistress at
Allenswood, on Eleanor

developed at Allenswood disappeared. She remained competent and took as good care of her family as she could, but she also became extremely serious and inhibited. As she later explained, she developed "an exaggerated idea of the necessity of keeping all one's desires under complete subjugation."

Eleanor Roosevelt officially entered society at the Assembly Ball at New York's elegant Waldorf Hotel in December 1902. "I do not think I quite realized beforehand what utter agony it was going to be or I would never have had the courage to go," she wrote later. "I knew I was the first girl in my mother's family who was not a belle and, though I never acknowledged it to any of them at the time, I was deeply ashamed."

Like other debutantes, Eleanor was enrolled in New York's Junior League, a charitable organization for wealthy women. Members of the league worked in hospitals or in settlement houses that served the immigrants who were pouring into the country. Settlement houses provided child care, taught English, and in general helped immigrants to improve their lives. It was just the sort of work Mademoiselle Souvestre thought people should do, so Eleanor took a job teaching children dancing and gymnastic exercises at the Rivington Street Settlement House on New York's Lower East Side. The work was very satisfying and gave Eleanor a sense of purpose during her family's difficulties.

Busy with volunteer work and the round of parties she had to attend, Eleanor still had time to see more of her handsome cousin, Franklin, who was then a senior at Harvard University. In some ways he was as coy and sheltered as she was. Franklin was intrigued by Eleanor's shy charm.

They courted according to the customs of the day. Eleanor later explained what had been expected, and revealed her own idealistic view of romance: "It was understood that no girl was interested in a man or showed any liking for him until he made all the advances. You knew a man very well before you wrote or received a letter from him. . . . You never allowed a man to give you a present, except flowers or candy or possibly a book . . . and the idea that

Eleanor's class at Allenswood during the summer of 1900. A charming and intelligent student, Eleanor (top, center) quickly became the headmistress's favorite and was, in the words of a friend, "the most important person in the school."

Crowds and commerce on Rivington Street, New York City, circa 1900. Eleanor worked on Rivington Street in a settlement house for immigrants as a member of the Junior League, a service organization for wealthy young women.

you would permit any man to kiss you before you were engaged to him never even crossed my mind."

Franklin, an only child whose father had died in 1900, was extremely close to his mother, Sara Roosevelt. She went almost everywhere with him, including on most outings with Eleanor. So under the jealous eyes of Franklin's mother, the couple began to care for each other.

In November 1903, after Eleanor had just turned 19, Franklin, then 21, invited her to Cambridge, Massachusetts, for the Harvard-Yale football game. Afterward the two of them went on what Franklin described in his diary as "a never to be forgotten walk to the river with my darling," where he asked her to marry him. Years later Eleanor confided to a friend that Franklin said he hoped she would help him to make something of himself someday. The idea of marriage seemed right to her and she was pleased "to be a part of the stream of life."

Eleanor with Franklin at his family's estate in Hyde Park, New York. Franklin was finishing law school at Columbia when they were married. He worked briefly (and unenthusiastically) as a lawyer before entering politics.

3

Wife and Mother

Eleanor and Franklin had many reasons for marrying young. For Franklin marriage would provide an escape from his protective, domineering mother. The marriage was also a political move for him within the family. Franklin admired Theodore Roosevelt, and had eagerly watched his progress through the ranks of political power. Theodore Roosevelt had moved from vice-president under William McKinley, to president upon McKinley's assassination in 1902. It delighted Franklin that his fiancée was the president's favorite niece.

For Eleanor, marrying early had other meanings. For one thing, there were few other choices for women of her day. Women were expected to marry and to raise families. But Eleanor was deeply attracted to Franklin. In many ways he was just like her father — a playful and enormously charming young man. He made her feel attractive, and took her away from the dreadful, competitive world of dances and parties where she felt like such an awful failure. But for Eleanor, getting married and starting a family glowed with promise. She would no longer feel like an outsider.

Cousin Eleanor has a very good mind.
—FRANKLIN D. ROOSEVELT
U.S. president (1932—45),
to his mother before his
marriage to Eleanor

The bride on her wedding day. Eleanor and Franklin were married on March 17, 1905. The bride was given away by her uncle, President Theodore Roosevelt, who then monopolized all the attention at the wedding reception.

Franklin's mother did not approve of the marriage. Though her letters cooed, "I am so glad to think of my precious son so perfectly happy," she also demanded more attention from him. She warned, "Don't let this new happiness make you lose interest in work or home." Franklin bargained with her. He told her he would go on vacation with her in the Caribbean if she would let him see Eleanor as often as possible in New York. Though Sara may have hoped that their trip together would change her son's mind, it did not.

Eleanor also tried to console her future mother-in-law. She promised to be loving and loyal. Franklin added his assurances in a letter: "And for you, dear Mummy, you know that nothing can ever change what we have always been and will always be to each other — only now you have two children to love and to love you — and Eleanor as you know will always be a daughter to you in every way." Eleanor visited Sara a great deal over the next few months and gradually entered the Delano circle.

In the spring of 1904, while Franklin was away, Eleanor visited Washington, D.C. She stayed with her Auntie Bye, her father's sister, and once or twice she was an overnight guest at the White House. Though she missed Franklin, Eleanor had fun. Not only was it interesting to see her dear uncle in action, but she was surprised to find she was comfortable with the leaders in the nation's capital. Her quick mind, eager curiosity, and lively conversation charmed diplomats, government officials, and celebrities alike.

The following fall Franklin and his mother moved to a rented house on New York City's Madison Avenue. Franklin began law school at Columbia University. In October he gave Eleanor an engagement ring. She longed to wear it but had to wait until they officially announced their wedding plans in December. After Uncle Ted's election to office the young couple was very much the center of the inauguration festivities in Washington.

Eleanor and Franklin were married on March 17, 1905, in New York City. The ceremony was held in adjoining townhouses on East 76th Street that be-

Eleanor with her future mother-in-law, Sara Delano Roosevelt. Rich and widowed, Sara focused all of her dominating personality on her only son, and did not approve of his marrying, although she acquiesced gracefully once the matter was decided.

THE BETTMANN ARCHIVE

longed to Eleanor's aunt and cousin. The rooms were filled with palms, lilacs, and pink roses. A rose-covered bower had been built in front of the fireplace to shelter the couple while they exchanged vows. Over the strains of the Wedding March, the guests in the elegant, candlelit drawing room could hear drums and cheering of the St. Patrick's Day parade. Yet the day had been chosen specifically because President Roosevelt would be in town for the parade and could stand in for his dead brother to "give the bride away."

In her elegant, high-necked dress of satin and lace Eleanor looked lovely. Some guests even whispered that she resembled her beautiful mother. However, the real center of attention at the wedding was the president. Lively and exuberant, all eyes were upon him. "Well, Franklin," he joked after the ceremony, "there's nothing like keeping the name in the family!" When Teddy Roosevelt strode into the library where the food was going to be served, everyone followed. Eleanor and Franklin tagged along behind their guests.

Not long after the wedding Franklin and Eleanor moved into a small hotel apartment in New York City, where they would live until Franklin finished his first year of law school. Eleanor furnished a tiny

Theodore Roosevelt waves to the crowd. The 26th president was immensely popular due to his boisterous, showmanlike approach. One of his children said of him, "Father wants to be the bride at every wedding and the corpse at every funeral." Franklin was a bit disgruntled to find himself upstaged at his own wedding.

room for her brother Hall so he would have a place to come to during vacations from boarding school.

The following summer the newlyweds went on a grand tour of Europe. Nearly everywhere they went, people fussed over them as family members of the president of the United States. Eleanor was surprised to discover how little she knew about government. When someone asked her to explain the difference between national and state governments, she could not. She decided to learn more about her country's administration when she got home.

Eleanor was not only naive, she was timid and retiring. Though Franklin invited her to join him climbing mountains, riding horses, and playing golf on their honeymoon, she usually declined. Terrified of looking awkward or inept, she refused to try and claimed that she was not physically strong enough. This inspired Franklin to call her "Baby," which he shortened to "Babs." He would call her that for the rest of their married life.

On the voyage home in late September, the young bride was miserable. She had never been a very good sailor, but this time she was truly wretched. The nausea continued even after the ship had docked, so Eleanor consulted a physician and found that she was pregnant.

While "the children" were in Europe, Franklin's mother had rented and decorated a little house for them on East 36th Street, three blocks away from her own on Madison Avenue. Everything was ready for the newlyweds when they arrived home. Sara had even hired servants. For Eleanor this proved both a blessing and a curse. Like other wealthy young women, she knew nothing about managing a household. Though her life was certainly made easier by having servants, and when the time came, a baby nurse, she failed to learn much about homemaking and child care. Years later, she regretted this and wished she had been a better mother.

Anna, the Roosevelts' first child, was born in May 1906, when her mother was 21. Eleanor hardly knew what to do with her. Not only had she never been interested in taking care of children before, she had never known any nurturing people, so she

had no one to imitate. Her shyness and fear of exposing her ignorance kept her from asking advice. Eleanor did not even have the courage to find out anything about birth control, so for the next ten years, as she wrote later, "I was always just getting over having a baby or about to have one."

The baby nurses and governesses did not keep Eleanor from worrying about her children. Anna and James, born the following year, were both small and fretful. They cried often and did not eat well.

Eleanor riding in a gondola on her honeymoon in Venice. Attempting to look candid and relaxed, Eleanor holds Franklin's straw hat while he takes the picture from the front of the boat.

Franklin, Jr., the third child, born just 15 months later, was as Eleanor put it, "the biggest and most beautiful of all the babies." He was happy and robust, but at seven months he suddenly died of influenza.

Eleanor despaired. She felt the baby's death proved what she suspected about herself — she was a bad mother. She blamed herself for having left the children in other people's care. She ached with grief and guilt. Even the discovery that she was pregnant again did not lighten her black mood. The new baby, Elliott, born in 1910, was frail and his legs were bowed. For months he had to wear heavy iron braces. Eleanor seemed unable to comfort the angry, unhappy child.

For a while, the young mother's life was quite restricted. At the time people thought pregnancy was more like an illness than a healthy condition, so she probably excused herself from most physical activities. In addition, Eleanor let her fears and self-consciousness govern her. She participated less and less in Franklin's world of pleasures, which included golf, sailing, horseback riding, and hiking.

Lonely and insecure, Eleanor became increasingly

The first new member of the Roosevelt family, Anna. Eleanor was to reproach herself later in life for being a poor mother. Comically, she once placed Anna in a wire cage to keep her from mischief, a strategy that scandalized the neighbors.

Eleanor (foreground) with a group of friends and local Indians at Campobello in 1907. A gift from Franklin's mother, Campobello served as a retreat for Eleanor, to which she returned frequently throughout her life.

dependent. Keenly aware of her shortcomings as a mother and homemaker, she still wanted her husband's and mother-in-law's approval. Perhaps they would love her more if she showed how much she needed them. Eleanor talked more and more about her weaknesses and asked for advice about almost everything.

Soon after James was born Sara decided that her son's family had outgrown their home, and decided to build them a new one, as well as a house for herself, on East 65th Street. Like the houses in which Franklin and Eleanor had been married, the new Roosevelt homes would be connected with sliding doors between them. Eleanor refused to be involved in the planning. Years later she confessed, "My early dislike of any kind of scolding had developed now into a dislike for any kind of discussion, and so, instead of taking an interest in these houses, one of which I was to live in, I left everything to my mother-in-law and my husband."

The result was disastrous. Only a few weeks after moving into the new house, young Eleanor Roosevelt sat at her dressing table and sobbed. She felt like a stranger in her own home. It was not where she wanted to live. After she calmed down and thought about it, she concluded that her own behavior had encouraged others to dominate her. She decided then and there to change.

I had high standards of what a wife and mother should be and not the faintest notion of what it meant to be either a wife or a mother, and none of my elders enlightened me. I marvel now at my husband's patience, for I realize how trying I must have been in many ways.
—ELEANOR ROOSEVELT
from her autobiography

4

Entrance into Politics

During the worst of Eleanor's depression after the death of her third child, Franklin decided to run for the New York State Senate. Two years earlier, during his first year as a law clerk in New York City, he had told his co-workers his dream of one day becoming president. Franklin had already mapped out the way to the top. First, he would win a seat in the New York state legislature as the representative from Dutchess County, where the family's Hyde Park estate was located. After serving in the state government, Franklin planned to enter national politics, perhaps through an appointment as assistant secretary of the Navy, a position his Uncle Ted had held.

In 1910, when the Democratic party in Poughkeepsie was looking for a candidate to run against a popular Republican senator and offered Franklin Roosevelt the nomination, he decided to run. The odds were against his winning, but the challenge appealed to him. He decided to mount an unusual campaign. At a time when automobiles were still rare, Franklin rented a flashy red touring car and hired a driver so he could visit, as Eleanor later

I thought that every government official investigated complaints and gladly tried to correct injustices. I realize now that this was a rather naive idea.
—ELEANOR ROOSEVELT
on herself as a
young woman

Franklin campaigning for the New York State Senate in 1910. Running as a dark-horse Democrat in a heavily Republican district, Franklin surprised everyone by winning. Eleanor can be seen in the background playing her part in Franklin's campaign, a role of increasing importance as the years went on.

described it, "every small four-corners store, every village and every town in Dutchess County. He became the first Democrat to win a senate seat in New York in 32 years."

Soon after the victory, the Roosevelts moved to Albany, the state capital. Eleanor was delighted to find that Franklin's mother planned to remain in New York City. For the first time in her married life she would not be ruled by her powerful mother-in-law. "I had to stand on my own feet now," she later acknowledged, "I was beginning to realize that something within me craved to be an individual."

Eleanor was not at all interested in politics herself, but dutifully learned about it because, in her words, "it was a wife's duty to be interested in whatever interested her husband, whether it was politics, books or a dish for dinner."

At 26, Eleanor Roosevelt was not a feminist. Many years later she confessed that she was shocked when Franklin came out in support of women's suffrage. "I had never given the question serious thought, for I took it for granted that men were superior creatures and knew more about politics than women did." Feeling she had little of her own to contribute, Eleanor tried to learn everything she could from other people. She was passionately curious, though sometimes her puritanical upbringing and rigid standards led her to misjudge others. "I found," she confessed, "that almost everyone had something interesting to contribute to my education."

One of the people Eleanor did not approve of at first was Louis Howe, an Albany newspaper correspondent, long experienced in politics. Howe was a small, untidy man with a deeply scarred face. His chain-smoking and often quarrelsome disposition irritated Eleanor. However, in time he became a trusted friend and was extremely important in shaping her political career.

In the three years the Roosevelts spent in Albany, Eleanor developed the skills she had shown in Washington before her marriage. She served her husband by researching issues he needed to know more about. She attended speeches and committee meetings, read documents, and explored the ideas and opinions of the many people who visited their home. Franklin appreciated her diligence and intellectual independence. Eleanor began to feel stronger. She also became more efficient in managing the household. She not only had to arrange everything for their home in Albany, but each summer she moved the entire household to Campobello, a Canadian island off the coast of Maine. The house, a barn-like, 30-room summer "cottage," had been a gift from Franklin's mother.

In the spring of 1913, after clearly indicating his interest in the position, Franklin was named assistant secretary of the Navy by President Woodrow Wilson. Nothing could have made him happier. Not only had he reached the second step in his career plan at the young age of 31, but ships, the sea, and

Senator Roosevelt and his family in 1910. Franklin was already being watched as a young man with a big future, which he pursued ambitiously. Eleanor was a dutiful wife, resigned to the constant change and insecurity of a politician's spouse.

A suffragettes' campaign booth in 1914. Surprisingly, Franklin was more committed to women's suffrage than was Eleanor at the time. Her contact, through Franklin, with the important political minds of the time was to nurture her development as a progressive thinker.

the Navy itself were among his greatest passions. He had collected and read nearly 10,000 books and pamphlets on naval affairs.

Franklin moved immediately to Washington. The family joined him after spending the summer boating, fishing, and picnicking at Campobello. The life of a Navy official's wife was very demanding. Protocol in the nation's capital was rigid, and though Eleanor disliked formality she did everything required of her. Monday through Friday afternoons she called on between 10 and 30 women at their homes. In addition, each week she held a formal open house for the wives of prominent officials. This left her only the weekends for the children. Though the demands seemed unreasonable, Eleanor conformed. "Nearly all the women at that time were the slaves of the Washington social system," she later recalled.

Eleanor not only met her enormous social responsibilities, but she entertained political leaders and other officials at home as well. Conversations

at the Roosevelts w~~ ~~
cause Eleanor liked to encourage people to say what
they thought. This not only earned her respect and
affection, but because she listened carefully, she developed an understanding of the government and
the social issues of the day.

To better understand Franklin's work, Eleanor
decided to accompany him on an inspection tour of
naval yards in the south. Not knowing the importance of details, she was impatient with his careful
examination of the rivets and seams on each vessel.
Franklin explained that the seams and rivets indi-
cated how well the ship had been built and main-
tained, which in turn affected the safety of the crew,
which finally determined the ability of the entire
Navy to defend the nation. The trip was an important lesson in how travel, observation, and good
questions could contribute to effective government.

Franklin came to be considered one of the most
attractive men in Washington. In contrast, Eleanor
paid little attention to her appearance. Though she
was tall and slender and had lovely reddish-blonde

Newly appointed as assistant secretary of the Navy, Franklin tours a shipyard with Eleanor in April 1913. The appointment was Franklin's choice as a reward for supporting Woodrow Wilson's presidential bid.

Recruits being mustered at Camp Upton, New York, during World War I. The United States had remained neutral for the greater part of the war, but by September 1918 more than a million American men were stationed in Europe.

hair and luminous deep-blue eyes, she did little to enhance her appearance. Instead, she soberly attended to what she considered higher priorities.

Franklin, always gregarious and fun-loving, was beginning to enjoy the attention of more confident and flirtatious women. To amuse himself he invited Laura Delano, an attractive young cousin, on the inspection tour with Eleanor. The two women were not at all comfortable together, but that did not seem to bother Franklin.

When they arrived home in Washington, Eleanor discovered she was pregnant again. As usual, she found the first months physically uncomfortable. She was probably delighted to have a social secretary she had hired a few months earlier help with the correspondence. Lucy Mercer, a young woman from an aristocratic family, fit easily into the Roosevelts' lifestyle. She was a charming, outgoing 22-year-old, whom the Roosevelts' son Elliott once described as "a lady to her fingertips." Three mornings a week she went through the mail and set up the calendar with Eleanor in the living room. She was also invited to luncheons and dinner parties whenever another woman was needed. Men enjoyed her company. She was pretty and easygoing. Franklin called her "the lovely Lucy."

That summer, Eleanor took the children to Campobello, as usual. Arrangements were made for doctors to attend the birth of the baby, due in August. Just a few days before the second Franklin, Jr., was born, the children's father announced that he was going to run for the U.S. Senate.

Again, it was to be a difficult campaign against a powerful incumbent, but this time he failed to win the election. After a demanding campaign schedule that took him away from the family for about six weeks, he was relieved to return to his post as second in command of the Navy in the fall.

Earlier that summer the fighting that came to be called World War I began in Europe. People everywhere across America argued about what the United States should do. Fairly early on, Franklin was convinced that the United States should join the Allies. Eleanor was not so sure. She did not believe war was ever a good way to solve problems and hated the idea of so many young lives being lost.

Eleanor and Franklin were divided in other ways as well. Their busy schedules left them little time to be alone together. Perhaps it suited them, for their social styles were very different. While Franklin was happiest when he was laughing and joking with friends or meeting people, Eleanor tended to be distant and formal. Luxuries like fine food and beautifully tailored clothes were pleasures to Franklin, but they were never important at all to Eleanor.

On the surface, life continued much as it had before for the Roosevelts in Washington. The children, or "chicks," as Franklin called them, were growing, and though they were mostly cared for by nurses and governesses, their mother planned their schedules and saw to their education. Eleanor had her sixth and last child, John, in 1916. According to Elliott, who later wrote a book about the family, he and James longed for the weekends when they could play with their father. "Pa," as they called him, was more fun and seemed to understand children better than their mother did.

Eleanor contributes to the war effort by knitting apparel for the soldiers. Other war work for stateside ladies included hospital visits, sales of war bonds, and relief work for widows and children left fatherless by the war.

5

Responsible Decisions

Life changed for Americans when the United States entered World War I. In Washington, the wives of government officials gave up their social schedules and began to take part in the war effort. Eleanor Roosevelt got busy as a volunteer. She helped start the Navy Relief Society and worked in a canteen in Union Station that served the thousands of troops passing through Washington each day. She served soup and sold candy and postcards. At home on the days she called "wool Saturdays" she distributed yarn to women she had enlisted to knit and collected the sweaters, socks, and scarves they had finished. Like many other women at the time, Eleanor became a habitual knitter. She did it whenever she had a spare moment.

With so much to do, Eleanor had to get her household to run more smoothly than ever. Looking after her family's needs and managing an ambitious schedule as a volunteer revealed an extraordinary talent that Eleanor called her "executive ability."

Every week Eleanor visited the young sailors and marines in the local naval hospital. Her genuine interest in people, her warmth and cheerfulness

One must never, for whatever reason, turn his back on life.
—ELEANOR ROOSEVELT

Eleanor and four of her children in 1920. The mood of the country had swung in the Republicans' favor, and Franklin for the moment left politics to work in a finance firm. For her part, Eleanor became involved in women's organizations, meeting the women who would later become her intimate network of advisers.

Eleanor and Franklin with his mother, Sara. During the stormy time of Franklin's affair with Lucy Mercer, Sara played a forceful role in keeping husband and wife together, threatening Franklin and offering encouragement to her daughter-in-law.

> There is so much to do, so many engrossing challenges, so many heartbreaking and pressing needs, so much in every day that is profoundly interesting.
> —ELEANOR ROOSEVELT
> from her autobiography

made her a favorite in the wards. She was especially distressed by the shell-shocked victims who talked to themselves and paced like caged animals. She was sure that in the crowded naval hospital they were not receiving adequate care. Eleanor decided to do something about it. She reported her concerns to the official in charge and recommended an investigation. To her great satisfaction, care in the hospital improved.

At night the Roosevelts continued to entertain Washington officials and foreign dignitaries. Eleanor was fascinated by the diplomats who came to Washington seeking U.S. support. With her knowledge of several languages and her ability to elicit people's opinions she explored alternatives to the values she had learned as a child. Years later, she explained in her autobiography: "Out of these contacts with human beings during the war I became a more tolerant person, far less sure of my own beliefs and methods of action but more determined to try for certain ultimate objectives. I had gained some assurance about my ability to run things and the knowledge that there is joy in accomplishing a good job. I knew more about the human heart."

Her own heart suffered painfully as she and Franklin seemed to drift further and further apart. In the summer of 1916, the year John, the youngest child, was born, she began to suspect her husband of having an affair with the young social secretary she had hired. That year, when an epidemic of polio, an infectious disease that usually crippled children, struck, Franklin had insisted that she and the "chicks" remain at Campobello until the end of September. Though she knew Franklin had a special dread of this disease and it was reasonable to keep the children from traveling through the states where cases had been reported, she suspected he had other reasons for wanting her to stay away.

Time passed and Eleanor kept her fears to herself. She and Franklin never really learned to talk about their relationship, so she could not ask him directly how he felt about Lucy Mercer, yet she was haunted with suspicions and their lives grew increasingly separate.

In 1918, when Franklin was asked to report on the needs of American troops in Europe, Eleanor decided not to spend the summer as usual with the children at Campobello. Instead she left them with her mother-in-law in Hyde Park and returned to Washington to devote all her energies to the Navy canteen.

In September her husband came home from Europe sick with pneumonia. While unpacking his suitcases, Eleanor discovered some letters from Lucy Mercer and read them. They confirmed her worst fears. The pretty young woman and her husband were lovers. Eleanor felt ugly, inadequate, and alone. Devastated, Eleanor offered her husband a divorce. That was what she wanted. However, in later talks it appeared that a divorce would not really

> *[Franklin] might have been happier with a wife who was completely uncritical. That, I was never able to be, and he had to find it in other people.*
> —ELEANOR ROOSEVELT
> from *This I Remember*

Lucy Mercer, the secret love of Franklin's life. Their affair was discovered by Eleanor, which caused tremendous tension and threatened to break up the marriage. The Roosevelts resolved to stay together, and their marriage became an unusual partnership, held together by affection and mutual goals.

Ground warfare on the western front during World War I. All told, 65 million men were mobilized and over 8 million died, in what was then known as the "war to end all wars."

solve anything because Lucy would never marry Franklin. As a devout Catholic she could never marry a divorced man.

When Sara found out that her son and daughter-in-law's marriage was in danger, she was outraged. Divorce was a disgrace she would not tolerate in the family. She threatened to stop giving Franklin money if he insisted on getting one. Louis Howe also warned Franklin that a divorce would destroy his political career. In addition, there were the children to consider.

By autumn, when the war ended, Eleanor and Franklin had resolved to stay together. Franklin and Lucy agreed never to see each other again, and a year and a half later, the young woman married a wealthy older man named Wintie Rutherford.

Less than a year after the crisis in her marriage, Eleanor's grandmother died. For her that death marked the end of an era, another break from the sad history of her childhood. Eleanor reflected that though she had never looked to her children for a sense of purpose or satisfaction the way her grand-mother had, she had wanted Franklin to supply those things. But at 34 she resolved to change. Many years later she described the kind of aware-ness she had in that moment to a young friend: "Somewhere along the line of development we dis-cover what we really are, and then we make our real decisions for which we are responsible. Make that decision primarily for yourself because you can never really live anyone else's life. . . . The influence you exert is through your own life and what you become is yourself."

American troops parade in Paris in July 1919, after the signing of the Treaty of Versailles. The treaty was harsh, stripping Germany of all rights and planting the seed for World War II. The first article, however, contained the charter for the League of Nations, which after a long struggle would become the United Nations.

6

Becoming an Individual

Still wounded by her husband's affair, Eleanor Roosevelt gathered her strength. She gave herself completely to her work with the Red Cross, her role as a mother, and her responsibilities as the wife of one of Washington's most promising politicians. She felt both stronger and more fragile than she had ever felt before. At home she was tougher and more decisive with the household help and the children, but with Franklin she felt clingy and tentative. In addition, she was suddenly at odds with her mother-in-law, who had been her greatest comfort and support during difficult times with Franklin. She could no longer tolerate Sara's sweeping judgments.

In 1920, when Franklin resigned from the Department of the Navy, the Democratic party nominated him to run for vice-president on the ticket with James M. Cox. Eleanor was glad for her husband, but dreaded the impact the honor would have on her life. She did not dream that the campaign would place her at the center of national politics.

Due to the ratification of the 19th constitutional

A new force appeared in the world . . . a woman who accepted personal responsibility for her country and her time — a citizen who took self government personally and seriously and would not rest until she had done what she felt she had to do.
—ARCHIBALD MACLEISH
American poet, on Eleanor

Eleanor with Marion Dickerman (center) and Nancy Cook, feminist activists in the Democratic party who became close friends and advisers to Eleanor. Eleanor came to depend on them for friendship and counsel throughout her life.

Franklin accepts the Democratic nomination for vice-president on the James Cox ticket, August 9, 1920. Running against Warren G. Harding, they represented a continuation of Wilson's policies, and a commitment to the League of Nations.

amendment in 1920, the election that same year was the first in which women could vote. Franklin's advisers recommended that Eleanor accompany him on a month-long train trip, campaigning across the country. The Roosevelts traveled in a private car with Franklin's staff; Eleanor felt out of place among his advisers. Louis Howe saw this and began to seek her out. He realized how intelligent and capable she was and knew that her husband's love affair had hurt her deeply. Sensing her need to be appreciated, he praised the excellent qualities he admired in her — liveliness, warmth, good judgment, and efficiency. Before long she was helping him to write Franklin's speeches and to manage the campaign.

While Franklin played cards late into the night with the rest of his staff, Eleanor and Louis enjoyed long, wandering talks about politics, communication, and hundreds of other subjects. Eleanor realized Louis was bright and sensitive and she began to share his enthusiasm for the game of politics. Through him she learned to appreciate the role of the press in a democracy and to enjoy reporters. By the end of the trip Louis and Eleanor were close friends.

That year, despite their efforts, the Democrats were defeated. The Roosevelts went back to New York City and Franklin's law practice, but Eleanor could not return to the social round of teas and luncheons expected of women of her wealth and status. Instead, she decided to join the League of Women Voters, an organization founded in 1920, which had fought for women's suffrage, and then direct its efforts toward improving working conditions for women and promoting participation in politics on the part of all citizens. Its members have rallied consistently for peace during wartime and for the rights of children. Eleanor was responsible for tracking the bills in the legislature that concerned the league. She soon distinguished herself as a clearheaded, serene, and efficient leader. Brilliant, independent women, like lawyer Elizabeth Read and her friend Esther Lape, a teacher and publicist, sought Eleanor's friendship. Their respect and affection helped to feed Eleanor's growing self-confidence.

Suddenly, in August 1921, disaster struck again. While vacationing on Campobello Island, Franklin became extremely ill. After a swim in the icy Bay of Fundy he developed chills, ran a raging fever, and his legs became paralyzed. For nearly two frightening weeks Eleanor nursed him almost constantly without knowing what was wrong. Doctors finally diagnosed the problem as infantile paralysis, or polio. He was rushed to a hospital in New York City.

Eleanor with Mrs. Cox, the presidential candidate's wife, reviewing a parade during the 1920 campaign. This was the first presidential election in which women voted, and Eleanor had been asked to join the campaign in part to appeal to their vote.

Though the first weeks were extremely painful, Franklin did not complain and was determined to remain optimistic. Louis Howe, who had practically become a member of the Roosevelt family, moved into their home to help. He, too, was convinced that "the boss" would get well enough to return to politics. Franklin's doctor also supported the family's optimism. A positive attitude could only help his patient.

Eleanor did everything she could to encourage Franklin's belief that he would walk again and to help him remain as mentally active as possible, but Franklin's mother opposed her. The older woman treated her son like a hopeless invalid. Tension grew between the two women. When Sara tried to rally the children's support, especially 15-year-old Anna's, by suggesting that Eleanor cared more about Louis's comfort in their home than she did for her own daughter's, Eleanor was furious. The difficult talk Eleanor had later with her daughter brought them closer, but she hardened her heart against her mother-in-law.

After long months caring for Franklin, Eleanor longed to return to political work. Louis told her that whatever she chose to do next would not only

Eleanor and Franklin on the campaign trail with advisers Louis Howe (far left) and Tom Lynch. Howe was a political scrapper whose rough manner at first put off Eleanor. Their association soon blossomed into a close friendship, and he was to become an important adviser to the future first family.

Franklin dedicating the new polio therapy center in Warm Springs, Georgia. In 1921 Franklin had become paralyzed suddenly by polio. Warm water therapy helped him (although he never regained full use of his legs) and he established a foundation to make it available to other victims of the disease.

help raise Franklin's spirits, but help keep the Roosevelt name in the public eye.

While casting about for a specific project to work on, Eleanor met Nancy Cook, the assistant to the chair of the women's division of the Democratic State Committee. She asked Eleanor to preside at a fund-raising luncheon. Eleanor was terribly nervous about speaking in public, but she agreed. Her quavering voice did not hide her competence and efficiency. It was not long before she was named financial chair of the committee.

Nancy Cook soon introduced Eleanor to her dear friend Marion Dickerman. Marion and Nancy had both been leaders in the New York suffrage movement. They came from wealthy old families like Eleanor's and shared her growing concern for social reform. During the next few years the three women became almost inseparable friends. Franklin would call them "the three musketeers."

With Louis's guidance and support, Eleanor worked not only in county politics but for the Democratic State Committee. Gradually she came to acknowledge her commitment to the ideals of the

Eleanor with Esther Lape, the intellectual feminist activist, and one of the women who formed Eleanor's circle of intimate advisers as she emerged from her husband's shadow as a progressive voice in her own right.

Democratic party. In an article called "Why I Am a Democrat," which she wrote for the *Junior League Bulletin*, Eleanor revealed how far she had come from the elitist ideals she had been taught as a child. "If you believe that a nation is really better off which achieves for a comparative few, those who are capable of attaining it, high culture, ease, opportunity, and that these few from their enlightenment should give what they consider best to those less favored, then you naturally belong to the Republican party," she wrote. "But if you believe that people must struggle slowly to the light for themselves, then it seems to me that you are logically a Democrat."

In 1922 Eleanor joined the Women's Trade Union League, a group founded almost 20 years earlier to help women workers organize for better working conditions. There she met and became friends with outspoken activists like Rose Schneiderman and Maude Schwartz, women with very different backgrounds from her own. Schneiderman, a Polish immigrant, was an impassioned speaker who, according to *The New York Times*, brought emotions "to a snapping point" after 145 women died in 1911 in a fire in New York's Triangle Shirtwaist Factory because their employer failed to provide for worker safety.

When Edward W. Bok, the former editor and publisher of *The Ladies' Home Journal* offered a $100,000 award in 1923 for "the best practicable plan by which the U.S. may cooperate with other nations to achieve and preserve the peace of the world," Eleanor Roosevelt became a member of the policy committee. The committee read and evaluated a total of 22,165 plans for establishing international peace. Though the work was exhausting, Eleanor was excited by it. She talked about all the best entries with Franklin.

When, as the contest rules stipulated, the winning proposal was to be presented to Congress, Esther Lape and Eleanor went to Washington to do it. The senators they approached refused to submit the plan. Eleanor despaired over their lack of courage and imagination. Though the Bok award did not

There is such a big, muddled world, so much to be done, so much that can be done if we increase in depth of understanding, in learning to care, in thinking of hunger not as an abstraction but as one empty stomach, in having a hospitable mind, open like a window to currents of air and to light from all sides.
—ELEANOR ROOSEVELT
from her autobiography

> *To me, the democratic system represents man's best and brightest hope of self-fulfillment, of a life rich in promise and free from fear; the one hope, perhaps, for the complete development of the whole man.*
>
> —ELEANOR ROOSEVELT
> from her autobiography

produce the new government policy its founder hoped it would, it provided an intensive education in the issues and politics of internationalism for two people who would become world leaders — Eleanor and Franklin Roosevelt.

In less than two years, the shy woman who once thought herself hopelessly inadequate had become a leader in New York state politics. Newspapers called her for statements, and she began speaking regularly in public and on the radio, so Louis Howe helped her improve her speaking style.

Eleanor, Nancy Cook, and Marion Dickerman traveled all over New York for the Democratic State Committee. They met with women, especially in rural areas, and convinced them of the importance of organizing. Even the men of the Democratic party were impressed, though Franklin was not entirely comfortable with her position in the limelight. Eleanor knew this and assured him in a letter, "I'm only being active till you can be again — it isn't such a great desire on my part to serve the world and I'll fall back into habits of sloth quite easily!" But this was clearly a façade. Like Eleanor's lifelong protests that she did not know what she was doing, it was an acceptable lie, a kind of personal cliché she used to draw attention away from herself. For by this time her political and reformist activities had become deeply important to her. They were not only at the center of the independent life she wanted for herself, but she could count on them to provide the greatest satisfaction she had ever known — the pleasure of helping others.

During his illness Franklin took on various nonpolitical jobs, including the presidency of the Boy Scout Foundation. For a few months a year he stayed in New York for these activities, but the rest of the time he spent in Florida, swimming and doggedly trying to strengthen his poor legs. His pretty secretary, Marguerite LeHand, or "Missy," as Franklin called her, an almost selflessly devoted young woman, accompanied him. Though it may have been difficult at first, Eleanor accepted this. She knew that she and Franklin had to develop separate lives.

Eleanor (standing, center) appears at the first session of the School of Democracy in New York in 1923. The school offered training in administration and organization sessions under the direction of the National Democratic Committee, where Eleanor was gaining prominence as a vocal leader.

7

Public Images, Private Lives

About the same time that Franklin began spending most of the year in Florida, Eleanor and her friends, Nancy and Marion, decided to build a house together. Franklin was pleased. He knew his wife had never felt at home in the big house at Hyde Park or any of the other houses his mother had arranged for them, and he wanted Eleanor to have a place of her own. He gave the three women a life interest in some of his family's land near a winding stream a few miles east of the big house and even designed a house for them. Val-Kill cottage, as they called it, was a cozy, fieldstone house, informal and welcoming. Nan and Marion lived there full time for many years and Eleanor joined them whenever she could. It was her favorite retreat.

Eleanor and her friends also embarked on other projects. Nan, who had once taught woodworking, suggested they start a factory where local people could learn to produce copies of Early American furniture. Eleanor and Franklin liked the idea. For some time they had been concerned about the great numbers of Americans who were leaving the coun-

> *Teaching gave her some of the happiest moments in her life. She loved it. The girls worshipped her. She was a very inspiring person.*
> —MARION DICKERMAN
> Eleanor's friend, on Eleanor at the Todhunter School

Eleanor at her desk in New York in 1928. By the time Franklin became governor of New York, Eleanor was prominent in the public eye. She published articles in magazines, reporters sought her opinions, and she was becoming a symbol for progressive American women.

tryside to work year-round in the growing cities. They hoped their factory might become a model for creating employment in rural areas. However, the project never became really profitable. It did employ local people through the 1920s and early 1930s and provided furnishings for the women's cottage and Franklin's house in Warm Springs, Florida. In addition, it produced hundreds of pieces the Roosevelts bought to give as presents for friends and foreign dignitaries.

Eleanor, Marion, and Nancy also purchased a small private girls' school in New York City. Marion served as principal. Eleanor became vice-principal and taught literature and history three days a week. The Todhunter School, as it was then called, drew most of its students from wealthy families. Eleanor wanted to change the way these girls saw the world. Patterning herself after her dear mentor Mademoiselle Souvestre, she became an inspiring teacher. She took her high school students all over the city. They visited tenements, settlement houses, markets, courts, and other places where they could learn directly about human needs. Eleanor loved teaching and believed in education. If people learned to see and think for themselves, she was sure they would want to do what they could to improve the world. When Franklin was elected governor in 1928 and the family moved to the state capital in Albany, Eleanor managed to fit three days a week of teaching into her busy schedule.

Franklin's victory caught her by surprise. Not only was she busy with Val-Kill and Todhunter, but in 1927 the Democratic National Committee had asked her to help organize women all over the country to work for Al Smith's presidential campaign. The task was enormous, but she agreed. When Franklin reentered politics and was asked to run for Smith's vacant seat as governor of New York, Eleanor was so busy that she had no time to help him. And though her friends told her what was happening in the race for the governorship, she was too busy to give it much thought. When at last the returns came in and Smith lost, Eleanor barely acknowledged the victory that others were celebrat-

Eleanor supervises work at the Val-Kill furniture factory in 1928. Created as a model for stimulating employment in rural areas, the factory never made money, although it supplied jobs for a number of local people.

ing — Franklin had been elected governor.

As usual, she found it difficult to adapt to the changes her husband's career imposed on her, but once the family was settled in the governor's mansion, Eleanor worked out a way to balance the demands of her official role with the activities she loved — teaching, writing newspaper and magazine articles, lecturing, and helping to run the Val-Kill furniture factory. The new governor's wife was es-

Eleanor stepping up for her first ride in an airplane in 1929. Air travel at the time was still viewed as dangerous, but Eleanor loved to fly and become a vocal supporter of the budding commercial air travel industry.

pecially delighted by her paid work. Without a college education, she was always a little doubtful about her professionalism. Eleanor loved the paychecks that confirmed the value of her work.

In addition to everything else she did, she continued to look after the comings and goings of her five children. By this time Anna was married, James was at Harvard, and Elliott and the two youngest, Franklin, Jr., and John, were at Groton, the boarding school all the Roosevelt boys attended. Even with her children so grown-up, she continued to think about parenting. Eleanor realized she had not been a very good mother. Though she had many good ideas about how to raise children, she was somehow unable to put them into practice. During the hectic days of the Smith campaign, she had written a magazine article about parental ethics. In it she urged parents not to be too critical or controlling, but to support their children in their efforts to shape their own lives.

As the wife of the newly elected governor, Eleanor was concerned that her success and visibility in New York politics might give the impression that she was more powerful than her husband, so she resigned from anything that might be considered politically competitive and sought ways to support him behind the scenes. However, when Franklin was unable to meet the physical demands of his job, she stood in for him. Though few people realized it, polio had left him completely unable to walk on his own. Eleanor took his place on official visits and inspections of state facilities, like hospitals and prisons. She became a keen observer and learned to interpret everything she saw. After each trip Franklin questioned her at length. Her reports helped him to improve the management of these institutions.

Because she traveled so much, Eleanor was assigned a security guard, a state trooper named Earl Miller. He was an energetic, handsome man, who was an expert rider and former amateur boxing champion. Though many of her women friends did not understand why, Eleanor enjoyed him and he became devoted to her. Earl was robust, cheerful, and flirtatious, and "the lady," as he called her, responded to him. With him she began horseback riding again, became a more confident swimmer, and even tried marksmanship. Some people believed Earl and Eleanor were lovers. Perhaps it was true. In many ways, however, they seemed more like sister and brother. Throughout their friendship Eleanor openly encouraged Earl's romances with younger women and even arranged for his wedding at Val-Kill cottage. In any case, he was part of the Roose-

I looked at everything from the point of view of what I ought to do, rarely from the standpoint of what I wanted to do. . . . I took an interest in politics. It was a wife's duty to be interested in whatever interested her husband.
—ELEANOR ROOSEVELT
from her autobiography

Eleanor with Earl Miller, a New York state trooper assigned to the governor's wife for protection. Miller became her constant companion for travel, sports, and relaxation. Speculations of a romance were almost inevitable yet unproven, but a deep attachment certainly existed between them.

velt's extended family for years.

Despite their separate personal lives, Eleanor and Franklin appeared to be a team in public. Though she was an increasingly powerful political leader in her own right, Eleanor chided those who suggested that she "wore the pants." Her contributions, however, did not go unnoticed. She used her position as an opportunity to help people. As the first lady of New York she became known as someone who cared deeply about other people's problems and did something about them. Letters poured in to her. She answered them and did whatever she could to alleviate the problems they described. Her compassion and effectiveness helped to win Franklin's reelection in 1930.

In some ways the Roosevelt partnership had an even deeper reality. Though their marriage was a failure by conventional standards, once they put

A family portrait from 1928. The Roosevelts' remarkable marriage had survived by adaptability. The future held many new pressures, but they were to last as a team, Eleanor serving as the crippled Franklin's proxy, while still pursuing many of her own interests.

aside the usual expectations and resolved to remain together to work to improve life for the average person, their affection for each other returned. The note Eleanor wrote to her husband the night of his reelection was a typical expression of her caring. "Much love and a world of congratulations," she wrote. "It is a triumph in so many ways dear and so well earned. Bless you and good luck these next two years."

By the end of Franklin's first term as governor the nation's economy was failing. Prices on the New York Stock Exchange had fallen dramatically the year before and thousands of investors had lost their money. They could neither pay bills nor buy new goods. Factories cut back production and laid off workers. One business after another closed, and unemployment spread like a plague across the land. Drought and dust storms were destroying crops in the Southwest and Midwest. For many people, the wave of hunger and poverty, known as the Great Depression, was inescapable.

By 1932 more than 25 percent of the workers in America were unemployed. Proud, hardworking people were reduced to selling apples and pencils on street corners and standing in long lines at soup kitchens for their food. As jobs disappeared families packed their belongings into their jalopies and moved on. They built shacks out of scraps wherever they went. In mockery of America's president, people called the shantytowns "Hoovervilles."

Republican President Herbert Hoover was caught in the flood of economic difficulties. Unable to do anything about them, he was losing popularity. While people wondered if a Democrat might do better, Franklin Roosevelt had been making a name for himself. His courage and charisma had won him a landslide reelection in 1930 as governor of New York, making him the Democratic party's first choice in their bid for the presidency in 1932.

Eleanor hated the idea of living in the White House and abhorred what she thought would be her narrow, ceremonial role as first lady. It was like being forced back into the gilded cage of social traditions that over the years she had fought so hard to escape.

What would her life be like if she could no longer enjoy the people and activities that had become important to her? Eleanor worried. Yet she worked hard for her husband during the presidential campaign. She organized thousands of women who went door-to-door all over the country talking about Franklin, and helped to produce the "Rainbow Fliers" they carried, colorful fact sheets describing the Democratic party's approach to various issues.

After Franklin's victory, she confessed to Lorena Hickok, a reporter assigned to her, "I never wanted to be a president's wife, and don't want it now." Eleanor Roosevelt was determined to remain herself. She told Lorena that Americans were not going to have an elegant first lady in the White House — "there is just going to be plain, ordinary Mrs. Roosevelt."

At first, as if to deny the change in her life, she kept doing everything she had done for 10 years — teaching, writing, speaking, and managing the Val-Kill factory. She accepted a contract to do a series of radio shows, wrote "My Day," a six-day-a-week column for newspapers all over the country, and

A dust storm sweeping over farmland at the beginning of the Depression. The stock market crash of 1929 and the subsequent economic plummet coincided with a killing drought. Desperate farmers lost their lands through bank foreclosures, and the country trembled on the brink of collapse.

I'd never have had the initiative or the ability in any one line to have done anything interesting alone.
—ELEANOR ROOSEVELT

73

Police maintain order at an emergency unemployment relief agency in 1931. Banks were collapsing and 15 million people were without jobs when Franklin was elected president in 1932. A year later FDR, as he came to be called, inaugurated the New Deal, a huge program to provide relief with public funds — radically close, some felt, to socialism.

edited a magazine. Later, as a concession to her husband's office she no longer did commercial radio work, and agreed to avoid political topics. Reluctantly, she also gave up teaching. But doing less frustrated her, especially when the nation was in such trouble, so Eleanor searched for a new project. She felt that presidents often lost touch with the public because they were bombarded by special interest groups. She knew that because people trusted her, they would tell her what was on their minds, and she felt she could help Franklin make better decisions. So when she asked if she could be his "listening post," she was deeply hurt that he thought it would interfere with Missy's job as his secretary.

Yet, Eleanor was determined to serve the country in some meaningful way. She knew she could make a difference. At a dinner given in her honor by the Women's Trade Union League, the organization she

had worked for in the 1920s, she outlined her intentions. "Perhaps I have acquired more education than some of you [who] have educated me realize. I truly believe that I understand what faces the great masses of people in the country today. I have no illusions that anyone can change the world in a short time. Things cannot be completely changed in five minutes. Yet I do believe that even a few people, who want to understand, to help and to do the right thing for the great numbers of people instead of the few can help."

The first lady ladles soup for unemployed women in New York in 1932. Small, practical gestures like this endeared her to the American public after years of President Herbert Hoover's chilly disdain for the common man.

8

A Singular First Lady

Eleanor Roosevelt changed the role of the first lady. Though she was expected to preside at important dinners, to entertain countless dignitaries, and to greet the thousands of Americans who came to see her, she remained herself, direct and unpretentious. More often than not she refused to ride in the White House limousine, or be protected by military aides or Secret Service agents. Instead, she walked on her own. Americans were "wonderful," she said. "I simply can't imagine being afraid of going among them as I have always done, as I always shall." People sensed her affection and trust and enjoyed her presence.

One day during her first months as first lady, she was taking her usual afternoon drive with Louis Howe when he directed her to an encampment of jobless war veterans along the Potomac River. The former soldiers were in Washington demanding a bonus payment from the Roosevelt administration. The previous year President Hoover had General MacArthur's army drive them away. The situation was sensitive, and Louis, who was now secretary to the president and jokingly called himself "the dirty-

Eleanor Roosevelt changed forever the role of political wives in the United States. We hold press conferences, make speeches, appear on television, assist in fundraising, and participate in all aspects of campaigning and the official life.
—HELEN JACKSON
wife of American Senator
Henry Jackson

Eleanor's 15-minute radio programs reached millions of people. At a time when the bewildered country more than ever looked to the government for leadership and help, Eleanor's reassuring presence made them feel they had an ally in the White House.

job man," was responsible for negotiating with them. He knew the effect his friend Eleanor would have, and since his health was failing, he decided to nap in the car and ask her to visit them alone.

The veterans were delighted to see her. Eleanor walked through the camp, chatting with them, and ended up at the mess hall. When they persuaded her to make a speech, she talked about the war and told them how much she admired the soldiers she met at the canteen. She had hated to see so many young lives wasted. In closing she said simply, "I never want to see another war. I would like to see fair consideration for everyone, and I shall always be grateful to those who served their country." Cheers and applause rang in her ears as she returned to her car. Not long after her visit, the veterans settled their grievances.

People in Washington were not the only ones to feel Eleanor Roosevelt's presence. Soon after his inauguration, FDR, as Franklin came to be called, sent her all over the country to find out firsthand how people were doing during the Depression. She visited the worst slums in the country, and inspected the federal work projects designed to start up the

Eleanor addresses the Bonus Army, a mob of World War I veterans demanding early pensions during the Depression. An earlier gathering had been dispersed by army troops under orders from President Hoover. Eleanor's visit was a great success, after which it was said, "Hoover sent the army; FDR sent his wife."

economy again. Americans saw her everywhere —
in cornfields on the plains of Kansas, high in the
cabin of an enormous crane over a dam that was
being built on the Tennessee River, and deep un-
derground in Ohio alongside miners in a grimy coal
car. Each hectic day on the road ended with Eleanor
alone in her hotel room typing reports for Franklin
and articles for newspapers and magazines.

Though she spoke personally with thousands of
people, she reached millions more in her writing
and radio broadcasts. Eleanor Roosevelt was always
in the news. Unlike her predecessors, this first lady
held her own press conferences. She took to the idea
as soon as her friend Lorena Hickok suggested it,
for she believed that communication in a democracy

**Eleanor visits San Juan,
Puerto Rico. She traveled
constantly during FDR's
administration, on her own
and as her husband's public
surrogate. By her own choice
she went to the most desperate areas, bringing encouragement and promises of
further action.**

Dressed as a miner, Eleanor rides a coal train to see first-hand the conditions in a mine. The country ran on coal energy at the time, but conditions in the mines were primitive and dangerous, causing constant labor problems. A visit from Eleanor meant that soon something would be done to alleviate the conditions.

should be as open and direct as possible. By inviting only female reporters to her weekly conferences, she encouraged newspapers to employ women and underscored her intention to focus on so-called "women's issues."

At first Eleanor spoke about topics like family life, health, and nutrition, and avoided political topics, but she could not resist speaking out against injustice. In her passionate desire to make life better for ordinary people she lashed out at the terrible conditions in factory sweatshops. She demanded an end to child labor and urged higher pay for teachers. She decried prejudice and discrimination against blacks. Her ideas shocked some people and offended others, and she was criticized for everything from her outspokenness to the way she dressed. Yet most Americans approved of her and felt inspired by her seemingly inexhaustible energy and goodwill.

When a woman Eleanor had never met wrote to say that she had come to think of the first lady as a friend she could count on in times of trouble, Eleanor was proud. She firmly believed that "the feeling that in the house where government resides, there also resides a friendship, is perhaps the greatest safeguard we have for democracy."

Eleanor's days in Washington were busy and long. She usually got up at 7:30, exercised or went horseback riding with Missy LeHand or her friend Elinor Morgenthau in Rock Creek Park, saw that Franklin's breakfast tray was brought to him, and visited briefly with her husband — all before she ate her own breakfast. After that, she met with the White House staff to plan menus and discuss the number of guests expected for luncheon, tea, and dinner. Tea was often served twice, at 4:00 and 5:00 P.M., to accommodate the hundreds of people who wanted to visit the White House.

Once the plans for the day were made, Eleanor tackled the mail. She received an enormous amount of it. During her first year in the White House more than 300,000 letters poured in. Eleanor answered thousands herself, and with her devoted secretary, Malvinia Thompson, she saw that practically every letter received a response.

She also wrote regularly to her children and friends. To them she wrote with a kind of breathless energy and passion, always telling them of her love and concern. It was almost as though nurturing others helped Eleanor to heal her own wounds. Writing late at night to her dearest friends also gave her strength and reinforced the loving personal ties that kept her from being engulfed by her public responsibilities.

Writing, like knitting during the war, was an activity Eleanor tucked into every free moment. For many years, along with her other work she met an ambitious schedule of deadlines for magazine articles and newspaper columns. To avoid criticism that she put her writing commitments ahead of her duties as first lady or misused government funds, she scrupulously restricted this "personal work" to evenings and weekends and paid her secretary from her own income.

As first lady, Eleanor traveled a great deal both for herself and for the president. She was very enthusiastic about air travel, even when planes were new

We have written the column while sitting on rocks, eating a picnic lunch, in a slowly moving automobile, on trains, in planes and on ships, once even on a destroyer.
—ELEANOR ROOSEVELT describing work she and her secretary did on the "My Day" column

THE BETTMANN ARCHIVE

"The Blue Eagle," symbol of the National Recovery Administration (NRA). The keystone of the New Deal, the NRA sought to stimulate business by promoting fair practices and price controls. Adherents earned the right to display the eagle, a subtle form of coercion on businesses who refused controls.

and most people were frightened to fly in them. Everywhere she went she asked people to take advantage of the opportunities the Depression offered them to help others, to work for the common good, and to change America from the competitive dog-eat-dog society it had become, into a more humane and cooperative one. She urged business owners to reevaluate what they were doing, to treat workers more fairly and to produce goods that were safe for consumers. She insisted that all people had the same rights to adequate housing and job opportunity regardless of race, and she protested the existence of laws that kept people of different races separated in schools, restaurants, and other public places. She objected to the government destroying

"Mopey Dick and the Duke," one of many cartoons aimed at Eleanor. Some critics felt that the first lady should confine herself to genteel activity in the White House; however, common Americans were delighted with their newfound champion.

LIBRARY OF CONGRESS

MOPY DICK AND THE DUKE

"Pull up your socks and straighten your tie, Duke, you can never tell when you'll run into Mrs. Roosevelt."

food to control prices when people were starving. And when the leaders of Germany, Italy, and Japan began to threaten the countries around them, she added world peace to her list of concerns. She believed that the United States should lead the way in establishing a safe and peaceful world.

Eleanor was confident that women and young people could play a great part in building a better world. The kind of world she envisioned would combine what she believed were the separate strengths of the two sexes, the "ability and brains of our men and the understanding hearts of women." She spoke at length to her husband about these issues, and partly because of her prodding, in his administration women occupied more important positions than ever before in the history of the U.S. government. The most prominent, perhaps, was Secretary of Labor Frances Perkins.

In 1934 Eleanor initiated a government program

Eleanor at the Vassar School of Euthenics, which taught progressive methods of child care. Remembering her own lack of preparedness for child-rearing, Eleanor promoted programs like this so other young mothers would be more prepared than she was as a young mother.

> *A great many government people to whom I referred letters regarded them as a mandate requiring prompt attention. Evidently they thought that if what I suggested was not done, I would complain to my husband. As a matter of fact, all I ever expected was that they would be interested in accomplishing the things that should be accomplished, since government is supposed to serve the good of the people.*
>
> —ELEANOR ROOSEVELT
> from *This I Remember*

for America's young people. She sympathized with their frustration with having very little meaningful work available to them. This program, the National Youth Administration, provided camping facilities, training, and jobs for many young people during the Depression.

At the same time, Eleanor helped women to assume greater leadership at every level in the Democratic party, but she warned that the women had better be talented because, as she put it, "during the next few years, at least, every woman in public office will be watched far more carefully than a man holding a similar position."

Louis Howe recognized the extraordinary talents of his friend Eleanor. Not long after Franklin was elected Louis strode into the first lady's sitting room, sat cross-legged on her daybed, and said, "Eleanor, if you want to be president in 1940, tell me now so I can start getting things ready." She dismissed the idea, saying that one politician in the family was enough. It seems, however, that her real reason was that she did not think most Americans were ready for a woman president. She hoped that someday they would be and that they would elect that person "as an individual, because of her capacity and the trust which a majority of the people have in her integrity and ability as a person."

As for herself, she was content to let Franklin be the politician if she could be "the agitator." People in political office seemed shackled by the voters' opinions of them. She wanted to be free to say exactly what she thought without worrying about how it would affect the public's response to her. She preferred to serve as a kind of conscience, an articulate source of suggestions and alternatives. Her words were the way to do this.

At every opportunity she discussed the nation's problems with Franklin. She showed him letters and constantly expressed her concerns. Many accused her of badgering the president and his top officials. They complained that it was hard to tell where her ideas left off and the administration's began. By the time Franklin was reelected in 1936, Eleanor Roosevelt's influence was felt throughout the federal government. She sent letters she received to the appropriate officials with notes of her own asking "What can be done about this?" or requesting a specific action. She invited government leaders and delegations of black sharecroppers or young radicals to tea. Some people, like Henry Wallace, the secretary of agriculture, disliked her and thought she was "a very dangerous person." She listened to their criticism, but did not let it keep her from doing what she felt was right. Even when she scored an obvious success, she refused to admit that she had any real influence. Whatever she accomplished was more the product of the circumstances in which she found herself, she said, than the result of her integrity or vision.

A picnic at Campobello in 1936. The country had begun to creep back to economic health under FDR's leadership, but the Depression was still on, and war was looming in Europe. The famous first family would have little time for rest in the years to come.

CALIFORNIA

9

A Friend in the White House

Though Eleanor found some aspects of her work as first lady satisfying, she disliked living so much in the public eye. She longed for a more private life, but her personal desires seemed trivial compared to the nation's terrible problems. She believed Franklin could do something about them, so she supported his campaign for a second term in the summer of 1936. Americans across the nation returned him to office in a historic landslide.

For the Roosevelts, however, the victory was bittersweet, because that spring Louis Howe, their friend and political adviser for more than 25 years, died. That small, frail, homely man had somehow managed to serve and befriend them both, even though their needs and personalities were extremely different. He had been an inspiration, instructor, and guide for two of the most powerful people in the 20th century. For the rest of their lives they would miss their devoted friend.

Friends had become keenly important to Eleanor since her disappointment in her marriage. Her private life was full of people with whom she could be

> She was the most famous woman of her time. But even that description hardly begins to encompass the extent of the affection and admiration that she stirred throughout the world.
> —New York *Herald Tribune*

Eleanor addresses the 1940 Democratic Convention. FDR's choice of Henry Wallace for his vice-president had caused an uproar; Eleanor's appeal to the convention to "rise above considerations which are narrow and partisan," proved sufficient to seal the nomination.

herself. Nancy Cook and Marion Dickerman had been among the first. Their friendship had been a haven for her in the heartsick days after she learned about Franklin's affair with Lucy Mercer. They had helped her to realize that she could have both a public and personal life that was rewarding. Lorena Hickok, the Associated Press reporter assigned to her during the first presidential campaign, helped Eleanor to adjust to her life in the White House. "Hick," as Eleanor called her, became one of Eleanor's most intimate friends. Her understanding and support helped Eleanor to expand the role of first lady and accept the part of the job she found so difficult — being Washington's official hostess. "Tommy," or Malvinia Thompson, who had started working for Eleanor in Albany, also became a close friend. This plainspoken, energetic woman was not only the secretary who "made life possible" for Eleanor, but served as a surrogate mother for the Roosevelt children, and became Eleanor's cross-country traveling companion. Even Earl Miller, who had married amid great publicity to squash rumors of his relationship with Eleanor in 1932, remained a lifelong friend. In her 60s she would make a new friend, David Gurewitsch, a physician nearly 20 years younger than she, who would also enter her circle of intimates.

Eleanor had other friends as well — Esther Lape, Elizabeth Read, Elinor Morgenthau, and Joseph Lash to name a few. Like the others, they nourished and supported her through crisis and change. They anchored her in her whirlwind schedule and gave her a new sense of belonging in the world. Many of them also informed and educated her about the organizations and movements they cared about, and provided an opening to them through which she could enter. As Joseph Lash explained in one of the many books he wrote about Eleanor Roosevelt, "Her relationship to causes and movements was through people. . . . Without people whom she cared about in a movement, she did not feel she understood it in its detail and complexity. And their genuine affection for her gratified her need to be of use, one of the governing principles in her life."

Eleanor worked for women's rights, youth, blacks and minorities generally, the end of poverty, and peace. Historian Mary Beard described her positions as reaching "the borderlands of political, social, and cultural change."

In an era when most people observed the "color line," the strict separation of blacks and whites, Eleanor Roosevelt boldly stood against racial discrimination and segregation. She entertained black farmworkers in the White House and visited them in their tar paper shack homes. In 1939, when po-

The great black singer Marian Anderson performing before the Lincoln Memorial. In 1939 Anderson was barred from singing in Washington's Constitution Hall because of her race; the alternate concert, which was arranged by Eleanor and others, drew 75,000 admirers, and Anderson was later invited to sing at the White House.

Eleanor and Franklin sharing a happy moment after Easter Mass in 1941. FDR had been elected for an unprecedented third term on his promise to keep the United States out of World War II. Yet Eleanor noted in her daily column that one can only promise to do one's utmost for peace — war might be inevitable, and so it turned out to be.

lice ordered her to sit in the "whites only" section of an auditorium in Birmingham, Alabama, for a public meeting, Eleanor defiantly moved her chair into the center aisle separating blacks and whites. A few weeks later she resigned from the Daughters of the American Revolution, an organization for the descendants of early patriots, when they would not let the black singer Marian Anderson perform in their auditorium in Washington, D.C. Soon afterward, Eleanor helped arrange a wonderfully successful outdoor concert for Anderson in front of the Lincoln Memorial. About 75,000 people attended.

Though Franklin was also concerned about racial discrimination, he was unable to take such strong positions. He was forced to be more moderate because he needed the southern leaders in Congress to support his economic programs.

Adolf Hitler and Benito Mussolini in Munich in 1938 for a four-power peace conference. The negotiations proved hollow, and Germany began its sweep across Europe, plunging the world into war. FDR was among those who had seen early that war was inevitable, and that U.S. neutrality must be coupled with preparedness.

UPI/BETTMANN NEWSPHOTOS

In the 1930s, while the United States struggled with its own internal problems, nations in the Far East and Europe began to expand their empires. Military leaders in Japan sent armies into Manchuria and China. The Italian dictator, Benito Mussolini, ordered his troops to take over the African nation of Ethiopia. Another dictator, Adolf Hitler, sent the German forces to occupy the Rhineland, Austria, and Czechoslovakia. Democratic leaders all over the world looked on in fear and horror and began strengthening their countries' defenses.

By spring 1939 Great Britain and France had joined together to form an alliance with Turkey, Greece, Romania, and Poland — the Allies. As Hitler prepared to conquer Poland, President Roosevelt and Neville Chamberlain, the prime minister of Britain, tried to discourage him from expanding his empire, but he did not listen. He sent his armed forces into Poland in September. Then France and Britain declared war on Germany.

Eleanor was alarmed by the prospect of another world war, but she strongly disagreed with Americans who protested Franklin's orders to strengthen the armed forces. Although she believed war was horrible and that fighting never settled anything properly, she had to admit it was time for the free nations of the world to join together and prepare to defend themselves.

The Japanese attack on Pearl Harbor took place on December 7, 1941 — "a date," said FDR, "that will live in infamy." A colossal blunder strategically by the Japanese, it stilled the voices for isolation in America, paving the way for the decisive commitment of the United States to enter the war.

In the shadow of the coming world war, Franklin decided to run for a third term as president, something no president had ever done before. At the convention in July 1940, he named Henry A. Wallace, a man unpopular with many Democrats, as his vice-presidential running mate. Delegates protested wildly and party leaders asked Eleanor to try to restore order. She stepped up to the podium and waited. In a moment the raging crowd of 50,000 delegates fell silent. Eleanor addressed them simply and without notes. She reminded them that in times of danger everyone had to assume greater responsibility. She urged the delegates to unite to help Franklin. "This is a time when it is the United States we fight for," she said. Soon after her speech the convention overwhelmingly nominated Wallace for vice-president.

Even after Franklin's reelection Americans continued to debate what should be done about the war. Amid heavy criticism, the president sent destroyers and war supplies to Britain. He also tried to force Japan to break its alliance with Germany and Italy by cutting off supplies of American gasoline, scrap iron, and other products. But the debate about whether the United States should remain neutral ended when Japanese forces attacked an American naval base at Pearl Harbor, Hawaii, on December 7,

1941. President Roosevelt asked Congress to declare war on Japan the following day. Overnight, Americans united behind him.

At the time, Eleanor was working for New York City's Mayor Fiorello La Guardia organizing the city's civilian defense, but once the United States entered the war she turned her energies to the national effort. She sold bonds, gave blood, helped the Red Cross raise money, knitted sweaters and socks, and visited troops in Europe and the Pacific. She saw firsthand the devastating effects of modern weapons.

Eleanor visited thousands of American soldiers. After talking with them, she often took their parents' names and addresses so she could let them know how their children were doing. All four of her own sons were in the armed forces, so she understood a parent's worries. Elliott was in the Air Force; James was in the Marines; and Franklin, Jr., and John were in the Navy.

Wherever she traveled Eleanor continued to write her newspaper column. She hoped it would serve as a link between Americans overseas and their loved ones at home. Most of the money she earned from her writing went to the Red Cross and the

Just before Pearl Harbor, when Mrs. Roosevelt invited me to come to Washington to help in the Office of Civilian Defense, she was under terrible attacks from many sides. I have never forgotten how she met friend and foe alike, apparently unperturbed by what people had said or done to her personally.
—JUSTINE WISE POLIER
U.S. justice

Eleanor visits Guadalcanal, scene of some of the most desperate fighting in the Pacific. Admiral William Halsey, after first refusing Eleanor permission to go, later chided himself when her visit accomplished a great deal more "than any other person who had passed through the area."

American Friends Service Committee, a Quaker organization working for peace.

Though Franklin was visibly exhausted by his work as president, he decided to run again in 1944. In June huge numbers of American and British soldiers had landed on the coast of France and driven the Germans inland. The Normandy invasion marked a turning point in the war, but Roosevelt felt he ought to remain in office until the victory was complete. He continued to work toward that end after he was reelected.

By spring 1945 the war was nearly over in Europe but the president's health was failing. He decided to go to his favorite retreat, the therapeutic spa he had built at Warm Springs, to rest. On April 12, a phone call to Washington brought the news of his death. Eleanor later learned that Franklin's old love, Lucy Mercer Rutherford, had been with him at the end. The Roosevelts' daughter, Anna, had secretly helped her father and Lucy continue their relationship.

Mourners along the funeral procession for FDR, who died on April 12, 1945. The president's health had begun to fail in the final year of the war due to age, chronic illness, and sheer exhaustion. He lived just long enough to see that Allied victory in Europe was assured.

Eleanor flew immediately to Warm Springs to make all the funeral arrangements. Returning to Washington on the train with Franklin's body, Eleanor felt numb. All night she lay in her berth with the shade open, watching the faces of thousands of people who stood along the tracks to pay their last respects to their president. Their grief seemed greater than her own.

Talking about her marriage at a later date, Eleanor said, "I think that sometimes I acted as his conscience. I urged him to take the harder path when he would have preferred the easier way. In that sense I acted on occasion as a spur, even though the spurring was not always wanted or welcome." Eleanor felt she was only one of many people who had served Franklin in his great drive to realize his plans for himself. Her life in the White House had not been her own. "It was almost as though I had erected someone outside myself who was the president's wife," she wrote later. "I was lost somewhere deep down inside myself."

A few days after Franklin's death a newspaperwoman stopped Eleanor to ask for a statement. Eleanor waved her away and said softly, "The story is over." But in fact, she would have more to tell.

The funeral of FDR in Hyde Park, April 15, 1945. Returning to New York, Eleanor told a reporter, "The story is over," but for her a new story was just beginning, starting with her appointment by President Harry Truman to the United Nations.

95

10

A New Career

Feelings of love, grief, and concern for the future swirled about Eleanor in the days after Franklin's death. Everyone seemed to want something from her. The new president, Harry S. Truman, sought her advice. Newspapers all over the world wanted her column. Others wanted a word of comfort or guidance. Her dear friend Hick tried to explain this in a letter, "You are like that — people instinctively turn to you for comfort, even when you are in trouble yourself."

In the midst of the hard work of moving out of the White House, settling her husband's estate, and turning the "Big House" in Hyde Park over to the government to become a museum according to her husband's wishes, Eleanor started writing her column again. She openly admitted that she was glad to be free of the restrictions of being first lady and looked forward to being on her own.

Eleanor decided to live part-time in the stone cottage at Val-Kill and the rest in a small apartment in Washington Square in New York City that she and Franklin had planned to use when they retired. By 1945 Nan and Marion had moved out of the cottage

The Almighty is trying to show us that a leader may chart the way, may point out the road to lasting peace, but that many leaders and many peoples must do the building.
—ELEANOR ROOSEVELT
from a "My Day" column
written shortly after
Franklin's death

Eleanor addresses the United Nations on September 16, 1947. In Truman's words, she was the "First Lady of the World," and he insisted on her participation in the UN delegation, where she served as a symbol of America's commitment to the organization's principles.

> *Mrs. Roosevelt brings to the Commission [on Human Rights] dignity, patience, prestige, breadth of understanding, genuine zest for the fundamental freedoms, and a revered name that is now historically associated throughout the world with the cause of human rights.*
>
> —CHARLES MALIK
> president of the UN
> Economic and
> Social Council

Eleanor and President Truman leave a memorial service for FDR on the anniversary of his death, April 12, 1946. After leaving the White House, Eleanor said, "For the first time in my life, I can say just what I want." She used her independent voice to promote peace above politics during the rest of her life.

UPI/BETTMANN NEWSPHOTOS

in Hyde Park, so Eleanor had it to herself. At first she was unhappy there. Though her relationship with Franklin had been scarred and was often strained, she missed him. Fala, his dog, became her almost constant companion. At times, especially when she was at odds with her children, she suffered terrible, almost suicidal, despair.

Hick frequently stayed with her, and other guests came to visit. Some were world leaders like Generalissimo Chiang Kai-shek of China; Princess Juliana of the Netherlands; Haile Selassie, the emperor of Ethiopia; Prime Minister Jawaharlal Nehru of India; and Ambassador Andrei Gromyko of the Soviet

Union. Eleanor also entertained groups of young people, like the boys at Wiltwick School, a local school for delinquent children. Food was almost always informal. Eleanor liked to serve her guests scrambled eggs, souffles, or picnic fare. Whenever possible everyone ate outdoors.

Because people everywhere recognized her, it was hard for the 61-year-old former first lady to have a private life, but on some level she did not really want one. She was already thinking about what she would do once she returned to public activity. Friends suggested she run for office, perhaps as senator of New York, but she refused. Politics never appealed to her. In fact, she did not even want to limit herself to working for the Democratic party, but she hoped she could invent a more independent way to serve the causes she cared about. For a while she concentrated on writing and radio work.

About eight months after Franklin died, President Truman asked Eleanor Roosevelt to be one of the American delegates at the first meetings of the United Nations. It was a role she had not imagined. "Why me?" she asked. Yet throughout the war she had been a leader in the peace movement. When the scientists who developed the atomic bomb urged the nations of the world to unite to control its use, Eleanor supported them. She did everything she could to further Franklin's efforts to establish an international organization to help maintain world peace. When the United Nations charter came before the Senate, Eleanor asked that it be ratified quickly so that the Allies could begin working together while they were still united in fighting the war. She even proposed Hyde Park as permanent home for the United Nations.

Yet when Truman called, Eleanor protested that she had no experience in foreign affairs and was unfamiliar with parliamentary procedure. The president ignored her objections and in the last days of 1945 she and the other American delegates sailed for London. On board she studied the armfuls of documents delivered daily to her stateroom, attended meetings and briefings by members of the state department, and whenever she could, sat in

I think I must have a good deal of my uncle Theodore Roosevelt in me because I enjoy a good fight and I could not, at any age, really be contented to take my place in a warm corner by the fireside and simply look on.
—ELEANOR ROOSEVELT
from her autobiography

with the reporters interviewing officials. It was just like being in school, and Eleanor thrived. For exercise, she walked the decks, usually arm-in-arm with someone whose opinions she wanted to learn. In the White House she had become very good at, as she termed it, "skimming the cream off a person's ideas."

Mrs. Roosevelt was assigned to Committee III, which dealt with humanitarian, social, and cultural matters. Delegates like Senator Arthur Vandenberg, a Republican member of the Senate Foreign Relations Committee, and John Foster Dulles, who later became secretary of state under President Dwight D. Eisenhower, considered this "a safe spot," where she could not do much harm. As time passed however, her hard work won her the respect of her critics. They came to call her "one of the most solid members of the delegation."

To everyone's surprise, an important debate arose early in Committee III. It was about the Soviet Union's demand that East Europeans who had left their homelands during the war return to them to live under Soviet rule. Andrei Vyshinsky, an extremely clever debater, spoke for the Soviet Union. Eleanor Roosevelt opposed him.

Vyshinsky, whom Eleanor mischeviously said looked "like a middle western banker," was the first to speak. He explained his country's position at length. It was nearly 3 A.M. by the time Eleanor was able to respond. She spoke briefly and with great conviction, arguing that human beings everywhere must have the right to choose where they live and should not be forced to live in a country where they would no longer be able to choose for themselves. When the vote was taken her position won.

Yet somehow Eleanor remained friendly with the Soviet delegate. Didn't opponents have to keep talking together if they were ever to come to any understanding? When the first round of meetings of the commission ended Vyshinsky asked Eleanor when she was coming to the Soviet Union.

Though the social aspect of diplomatic work did not appeal to her, she had learned to enjoy observing people. The manners and vanity of some of the del-

egates amused her. Some she found rude and arrogant, while others seemed excessively cordial. "I'm so glad I never feel important," she wrote to one of her UN colleagues, "it does complicate life!"

The summer after the first meetings of the Human Rights Commission, Eleanor began writing her autobiography. The process was difficult, she said, because it was boring to write about herself. One day, driving south from Hyde Park she had a car accident. Eleanor was badly bruised and her front teeth were broken. To her delight, they were replaced by "two lovely porcelain ones," which did not protrude as her own teeth had. By October she was well enough to attend the opening sessions of the General Assembly. Still dressed in black in memory of her husband, and carrying her old briefcase, Eleanor returned to her UN diplomatic work.

In her role as U.S. delegate to the UN, Eleanor often found herself having to do battle on several fronts. When she could not support the official position she had been given as a delegate, she fought with her advisers in the State Department and the White House to change it. She continued to help shape U.S. government policy. For example, in March 1948, when the U.S. failed to be as generous in its support for Israel as she thought it should be, she sent a note to President Truman threatening to resign her position as "a small cog in our work at the UN." Not long after, U.S. aid to Israel increased.

The members of the United Nations Commission on Human Rights, April 30, 1946. Eleanor was chair of the commission while they hammered out a universal declaration of rights, and she worked for years afterwards to make it a binding covenant among nations.

On the streets of New York with FDR's beloved dog, Fala. After FDR's death, Eleanor had looked forward to a quiet retirement of writing. In fact, she became busier than ever, touring the world for the cause of human rights.

Throughout her seven years as a UN delegate she insisted that the United States make a greater effort to understand the traditions and interests of other nations. "We're not living in an American world," she reminded her advisers. She also worked to enlarge and increase the humanitarian work of many organizations within the UN. When cold war tensions increased during the 1950s and the Soviet Union and the United States threatened to fight each other, she was frustrated that the UN was unable to play a greater role in maintaining world peace. She proposed that all countries hand over their weapons to the UN for safekeeping, but members of her own delegation refused to consider it.

When Dwight D. Eisenhower became president in 1953, Eleanor resigned so that he could choose his own representative. He did not reappoint her. However, eight years later, President John F. Kennedy returned her to the diplomatic post. When she arrived to take her seat, the delegates from the other nations stood and applauded her. This had never happened before at the UN, and it was one of the proudest moments of her life.

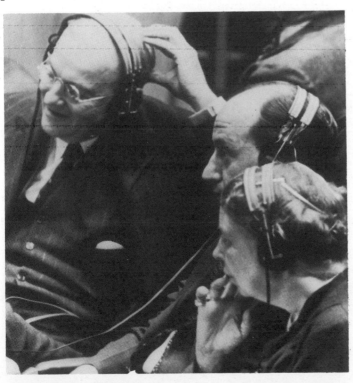

Eleanor with Adlai Stevenson and John Foster Dulles at the United Nations in 1946. Stevenson was a senior adviser to the first General Assembly, and later ran for president with Eleanor's support, losing twice to Dwight D. Eisenhower.

11

Fighting On

After World War II, powerful anticommunist feelings raged over the country. Led by Wisconsin Senator Joseph McCarthy, many Americans came to believe that communists were behind the United States' loss of world power. Almost everyone in public life was suspected of being a communist or being influenced by them.

Eleanor was appalled to find Americans afraid to criticize their government, to attend protest meetings, or to take other political action for fear of being accused of having communist affiliations. "In a democracy you must be able to meet with people and argue your point of view — people whom you have not screened beforehand. That must be part of the freedom of people in the United States." In her column she wrote, "Either we are strong enough to live as a free people or we will become a police state. There is no such thing as being a bystander on these questions."

She had also refused to retreat before the attacks of Cardinal Spellman, America's most powerful Catholic leader. Spellman had tried to drive her out of public life because she opposed federal aid for

> *You gain strength, courage, and confidence by every experience in which you really stop to look fear in the face. You must do the thing which you think you cannot do.*
> —ELEANOR ROOSEVELT

Eleanor Roosevelt in the early 1960s. Given the world situation, she said, "there is no such thing as being a bystander," and she kept up her grueling schedule of appointments, official visits, and Democratic party activities until her death at age 77.

Senator Joseph McCarthy with attorney Roy Cohn during the hearings held in 1954 to investigate the senator's conduct. McCarthy destroyed dozens of careers in the early 1950s with his reckless accusations of communism. Until his censure by Congress, only the most independent voices, including Eleanor Roosevelt, dared attack him publicly.

parochial schools, supported birth control, and took other outspoken positions. Her own lack of desire for power seemed to make her invulnerable. In the face of the most vicious attacks she simply claimed she would withdraw from public life if opposition to her views became a real problem. For her the most distressing part of such criticism was its effect on her children.

Critics, though, were in the minority. In 1951, readers of a newspaper poll in Texas named Eleanor Roosevelt "the greatest living American woman." Her strong, ubiquitous presence made her a national symbol. As cold war tensions escalated and the Soviets portrayed the United States as an aggressive, power-hungry nation, Mrs. Roosevelt's intelligence and compassion seemed to reassure people all over the world about America's intentions. Eleanor, however, was deeply worried about her own country's increasing militarism.

At about the same time, the State Department realized her potential as an ambassador and urged her to visit the Middle East, India, and Pakistan as a writer. Almost everywhere she went, huge crowds appeared. People cheered or knelt as she passed. Eleanor attributed these demonstrations to respect for her late husband. After her travels Eleanor met with U.S. government officials to share her observations of life in developing countries. She also wrote a book for the general public.

Though she tried to stay out of national politics, Eleanor was unable to refuse former President Truman's invitation to speak about the importance of the United Nations at the Democratic convention in Chicago in July 1952. Thousands of delegates stood and cheered when she arrived. Again Eleanor insisted the standing ovation was for Franklin.

During the convention the Democrats nominated Adlai Stevenson, governor of Illinois, to run for president against the incumbent Republican president and former war hero, Dwight D. Eisenhower. Eleanor knew Stevenson from her work with him at the UN. His wit and clarity delighted her. She wanted to help him, but decided to limit her political appearances. Her praise rang out in her columns.

"He knows more about the world than almost any other man in this country," she wrote. She was deeply disappointed when Stevenson was defeated but decided to go all out to help him if he decided to run again in 1956.

When Eleanor Roosevelt left the United Nations she started working with a nongovernmental organization, the American Association for the United Nations. She traveled all over the United States to build support and raise funds for the organization. She also accepted the honorary chairmanship of Americans for Democratic Action, a progressive organization she had long supported. The group needed someone willing to oppose Senator Joseph McCarthy's anticommunist campaign.

During the 1950s Eleanor continued to visit other countries. In 1952 she was invited to visit Japan. After that she went to Hong Kong, Turkey, and Greece. She also met with Marshal Josip Broz Tito, the ruler of Yugoslavia, whose personality and government fascinated her. Five years later when the *New York Post* asked Roosevelt, age 73, to go to China and the Soviet Union as a reporter, she was delighted. For years she had longed to go to the Soviet Union. She firmly believed that if Americans and Russians knew more about each other, great strides would be made in the struggle for world peace. The trip to the USSR was one of the most

'You really must slow down.' This is becoming the repeated refrain of my children and all of my friends. But how can I when the world is so challenging in its problems and so terribly interesting?
—ELEANOR ROOSEVELT
from her autobiography

Eleanor meeting Soviet Premier Nikita Khrushchev on her visit to the Soviet Union in 1957. "The time to work for peace," she said, "is when you are at peace. When the die is cast, it is too late to do anything."

important, exciting, and informative journeys of her entire life.

Eleanor, always intensely curious, was frustrated, at first, by the Soviet government's efforts to limit what she saw of the country. She also found it difficult to get reliable statistics for her stories. But as she attended ballets and circuses, visited museums, farms, cathedrals, and villages in central Asia, she tried to see them through Russian eyes.

The highlight of her tour was a meeting with Nikita Khrushchev, the new Soviet premier, at his villa near Yalta on the Black Sea. For two and a half hours they discussed through interpreters the Cold War, the arms race, and the violation of the peace agreements. They disagreed passionately about the causes of these problems and their conversation became heated at times, but by the end of the visit they had shared a meal and learned a great deal about each other.

"Can I tell our papers that we have had a friendly conversation?" Khrushchev asked.

"You can say that we had a friendly conversation but that we differ," Eleanor replied firmly.

Her host laughed and replied, "At least we didn't shoot each other."

Her visit to the Soviet Union inspired Eleanor to keep trying to improve relations between the United States and the Soviet Union. Every time the Soviet premier was in the United States she invited him to Hyde Park, even in 1960, after he had angrily attacked the United States in the UN. When she was criticized for entertaining him, Eleanor said, "We have to face the fact that either all of us are going to die together or we are going to learn to live together and if we are to live together we have to talk."

In the late 1950s Eleanor began to have health problems. In 1960 David Gurewitsch, her friend and the only physician she trusted, diagnosed her condition as aplastic anemia, a disease of the bone marrow. It would shorten her life. Eleanor's approach to her illness was to ignore it. She shrugged off the fevers, aches, and pains because she believed that paying attention to them was the first step to becoming an invalid.

She continued to remain very active. She tried and failed to convince the Democratic party to nominate Adlai Stevenson again as its presidential candidate in 1960. With reluctance, she supported their nominee, John F. Kennedy. In time, however, she became Kennedy's friend and adviser. When the U.S.-sponsored Bay of Pigs invasion of Cuba in 1961 failed, she helped to negotiate the exchange of prisoners with Fidel Castro. She served on the National Advisory Council of the Peace Corps and devoted a great deal of time to promoting the work of the United Nations.

Eleanor also worked in politics on a local level. With Herbert H. Lehman, Robert Wagner, and others, she campaigned fiercely to free the Democratic party in New York from the control of big bosses like Carmine De Sapio.

Eleanor with Golda Meir, prime minister of Israel, in 1960. Eleanor was a staunch supporter of Israel; in 1948 she had threatened to resign as UN delegate if U.S. aid to the newly established nation was not increased. Of the Israelis, Eleanor said, "They will survive because of their leadership."

Eleanor with President John F. Kennedy, discussing his fledgling Peace Corps program. Eleanor saw the Peace Corps as another way to cement America's relations with the rest of the world — a vital element, in her mind, to continued peace.

> *If she were alive today, [my mother] would have worked for the passage of the Equal Rights Amendment to the Constitution. Her argument would have been that women had a right and duty to work side by side with men in all phases of life.*
> —ELLIOTT ROOSEVELT

In addition, she lectured, became a professor at Brandeis University, and did a television series called "The Prospects of Mankind." She cut back her newspaper columns to three a week and began work on another book, *Tomorrow Is Now*, a challenge to America's younger generation and a call for responsible leadership in a complex world. In the midst of it all, she knew she was dying and prepared for it by writing directions for the kind of funeral she wanted and sending checks in advance to the people and causes she wanted to support.

In July 1962 Eleanor became too sick to continue her activities. She hated to give in to illness, and despised being hospitalized for what seemed endless tests and injections. By the end of October, doctors found the problem was a rare form of tuberculosis of the bone marrow and changed their treatment, but she failed to respond. Eleanor hated the indignities of being in the hospital. Though she was exhausted by the illness and drifted in and out of consciousness, she was determined to die at home. Her children brought her back to her little house in New York City and stayed with her until she died on November 7, 1962.

Eleanor Roosevelt is best remembered for her strong belief that the rights of the individual correspond directly to the well-being of the country and the world. In 1958, four years before her death, she observed in a speech at the UN: "Where, after all, do universal rights begin? In small places, close to home — so close that they cannot be seen on any maps of the world. Yet they are the world of the individual person; the neighborhood he lives in; the school or college he attends; the factory, farm, office where he works. Such are the places where every man, woman, and child seeks equal justice, equal opportunity, equal dignity without discrimination. Unless these rights have meaning there they have little meaning anywhere. Without concerned citizens' action to uphold them close to home, we shall look in vain for progress in the larger world."

Eleanor addressing the Democratic National Convention in 1960. Eleanor had become a respected representative and symbol of the Democratic party. Though she initially supported Adlai Stevenson, she switched her endorsement to the party's choice, Kennedy, to promote Democratic unity and ensure the return of a Democrat to the White House.

Further Reading

Blassingame, Wyatt. *Eleanor Roosevelt.* New York: G. P. Putnam's Sons, 1967.

Hickok, Lorena A. *The Story of Eleanor Roosevelt.* New York: Grosset & Dunlap, 1959.

———. *Eleanor Roosevelt: Reluctant First Lady.* New York: Dodd, Mead & Company, 1962.

Hoff-Wilson, Joan, and Marjorie Lightman, eds. *Without Precedent: The Life and Career of Eleanor Roosevelt.* Bloomington: Indiana University Press, 1984.

Lash, Joseph P. *"Life Was Meant to Be Lived": A Centenary Portrait of Eleanor Roosevelt.* New York: W. W. Norton & Co., 1984.

Roosevelt, Eleanor. *This I Remember.* New York: Harper & Brothers Publishers, 1949.

———. *The Autobiography of Eleanor Roosevelt.* New York: Harper & Brothers Publishers, 1961.

———. *Tomorrow Is Now.* New York: Harper & Row, 1963.

Roosevelt, Elliott. *Eleanor Roosevelt, with Love: A Centenary Remembrance.* New York: E. P. Dutton, 1984.

Chronology

Oct. 11, 1884	Anna Eleanor Roosevelt born in New York City
1892	Death of Eleanor's mother and brother Elliott, Jr.
1894	Death of Eleanor's father
1899–1902	Eleanor attends Allenswood, an English school for girls
March 17, 1905	Marries her distant cousin, Franklin Delano Roosevelt
1906	Birth of the Roosevelts' first child; over the next ten years, Eleanor gives birth to six children, five of whom survive infancy
1920	Eleanor joins the League of Women Voters; and subsequently becomes involved in Democratic party politics and women's organizations
Aug. 1921	Franklin is stricken with polio, which leaves him crippled
1927	Eleanor buys the Todhunter School, where she serves as vice-president and teaches literature and history
1928	Franklin becomes governor of New York; Eleanor makes frequent fact-finding trips for her husband
1932–45	Franklin serves as president of the United States; as first lady, Eleanor works for the rights of women and minorities, anti-poverty programs, and world peace
1934	Eleanor helps launch the National Youth Administration, which provides jobs and training for young people
1936	Begins publishing her newspaper column, "My Day"
1939–45	World War II
1941–42	Eleanor serves as assistant director of civilian defense in New York City
April 12, 1945	Franklin dies
1945	President Truman appoints Eleanor as delegate to the United Nations (UN)
1946–51	Serves as chair of the UN Human Rights Commission
Dec. 10, 1948	After years of lobbying, the International Declaration of Human Rights, which Eleanor co-drafted, is adopted by the UN
1952	Eleanor represents the U.S. State Department in India, Pakistan, and the Middle East
1953	President Eisenhower fails to reappoint Eleanor to the UN Eleanor travels to Hong Kong, Turkey, Greece, and Yugoslavia
1957	Meets with Premier Khrushchev in the USSR
1961	Reappointed to the UN by President Kennedy
Nov. 7, 1962	Dies of tuberculosis

Index

Karen McAuley, a graduate of Bennington College in Vermont, taught junior high school students for nine years in and around New York City. She is currently a freelance writer specializing in educational materials, and has written several books, including the *Golda Meir* volume in the Chelsea House series WORLD LEADERS   PAST & PRESENT.

Arthur M. Schlesinger, jr., taught history at Harvard for many years and is currently Albert Schweitzer Professor of the Humanities at City University of New York. He is the author of numerous highly praised works in American history and has twice been awarded the Pulitzer Prize. He served in the White House as special assistant to Presidents Kennedy and Johnson.